Praise for *We're All In*

"Robert Mixon speaks with the rare combination of authority and humility that has marked his leadership since our days together at West Point. *We're All In* persuades us that culture defines our organizations and either unleashes or stifles the potential of each individual. Those who aspire to lead must have this book in their leadership tool bag."

General (Retired) Martin E. Dempsey, United States Army
18th Chairman of the Joint Chiefs of Staff

"Robert Mixon's *We're All In* is a superb primer for effecting change in an organization. My leadership team initiated our annual strategic planning process with General Mixon's five levels to excellence in culture as a guide."

Patrick McBrayer, President & CEO
ACell, Inc.

"Robert Mixon clearly understands what makes great cultures come to life, and the elegance of *We're All In* lies in its simplicity and the practical tools he provides to take your culture to a level of excellence your competitors won't be able to touch. His proven leadership at the highest levels of military and corporate organizations is but one indicator of his keen understanding of what it takes to build and sustain world-class cultures. I highly recommend this book be on the desk of every leader, at every level, including those who aspire to lead."

F. William Smullen, Author and Lecturer
Director of National Security Studies, Syracuse University

"We're All In is an excellent book on how organizations from both the public and private sector can improve their organizational culture. The book has exceptional examples, ideas, and a deliberate process to help leaders get to a Level 5, world-class culture."

General (Retired) Keith Alexander, United States Army

"A healthy culture is absolutely crucial to organizational success. Level 5 culture enables organizations to be the very best. This outstanding book provides the proven framework to get you there in an easy to understand and methodical way. It will transform your company!"

David Pinder, President
Cardinal Glass Industries

"Major General Robert Mixon has captured all of the critical components of a world-class culture in this very useful, powerful book. His unique blend of executive experience in both military and corporate organizations, and his extensive background studying and assisting a variety of different companies and their cultures, makes him a true subject matter expert. Any type of organization, large or small, will benefit tremendously from reading and implementing the tools Robert describes in *We're All In."*

General (Retired) Walter "Skip" Sharp, United States Army

"Robert Mixon has authored an insightful book on building a high functioning, successful culture. All leaders will benefit by applying its lessons. I wish I read it earlier in my career as it no doubt would have helped me develop a great company sooner than later. A must read!"

Frank A. Insero, Managing Partner
Insero Wealth Strategies

"Wow! As a General Officer and corporate executive, Robert has a full range of cultural experience...good and bad. *We're All In* provides a fast-paced guide to evaluate your culture and then practical steps for moving it to World-Class. I could have used his insights, methods and mentorship when developing our world-class culture at Mustang Engineering. Robert helps you create an "ALL IN" culture that will dominate your industry and take care of people long term. Get this book and start the rewarding journey today!"

Bill Higgs, labeled "King of Culture" by Upstream Magazine
Author: *Mustang, The Story*

"We're All In should be a desk-side reference for every leader, at every level, in every organization."

Jeff Nix, Assistant General Manager
Detroit Pistons

"Robert has captured simple learnings from his military and corporate experiences in *We're All In* to help others understand and establish peak performance organizations by developing level 5 cultures. Robert has developed a simple formula informed through his experiences explained by his Big Six Principles. Anyone in a leadership role aspiring to create a world class culture must read this book and apply these principles! Your people want it and your customers deserve it!"

Timothy C. Tyson, Chairman & CEO
Avara Pharmaceutical Services

"This book brings such an awareness of culture that it compels you to desire a world-class culture in every team of which you are a part. General Mixon's "Six Leadership Principles" integrated into his book are a must-read for present and future profit, nonprofit, mid- and C-level Executives. SMU-Cox Business Leadership Center, MBA students, and organizations that hire these graduates have benefited greatly from General Mixon's "Six Leadership Principles" program, where he's shared his wisdom and insight."

Paula (Hill) Strasser, Adjunct Faculty, Director
MBA Business Leadership Center
& Edwin L. Cox BBA Business Leadership Institute
SMU-Cox School of Business

WE'RE ALL IN

The Journey to a World-Class Culture

Robert W. Mixon, Jr. Major General (USA, Retired)

Level Five Associates
VALUES BASED LEADERSHIP THAT WORKS

Contents

Foreword

When I first met Robert Mixon more than 10 years ago, I had no idea we would develop a lifetime friendship. That's exactly what's happened. What was immediately clear to me at that time was that he was a unique individual, a leader who understood people and had a way of communicating that separated him from others. He was an Army General who didn't act like he was in command of thousands of soldiers and civilians. He was just Robert.

Since his retirement from the military after 33 years of service, Robert has now spent a decade in the "corporate world." There he has continued to excel as an executive in both for-profit and not-for-profit companies, using his same extraordinary communication skills to lead others to success. He understands what makes great organizations come to life.

In my 37-year basketball career in coaching and as an executive at the collegiate and professional levels, I have seen great teams and unsuccessful teams. The key differentiator is effective leadership, which creates the conditions for a world-class culture. The difference between a winning and losing team is dependent on leadership at every level — ownership, management, coaches and the players. I have experienced both sides, and nothing beats the feeling within an organization when everyone is pulling in the same direction. At the end of the day, it's the leadership of all facets of an organization that eventually flows to the players and culture of the locker room that can dictate the direction of the team.

Great teams always have a coach who allows a player or players to take command of the locker room and provide leadership on and off the court. I've experienced vocal leaders and ones who did not display a verbal presence but led by example. Both were effective, and the respect earned from fellow teammates drove success. Robert used his experiences through the years to evaluate, coach, and develop the same type of leaders for his team in the United States Army.

Winners live in a culture where the team is more important than any individual, and that's what this book is all about. It's about trusting the person on the right and left of you with the understanding that they know it's not about them, and all involved want to be a piece of the puzzle for success. My experiences in winning and losing have been on a basketball court. Important yes, but it's just a game. Robert's success in leadership and his command of several thousand troops are centered on an effective mission with all of his soldiers returning safely in good health. His game is the game of life, and his leadership qualities are instilled in his troops to create a positive operational culture.

In this book, Robert has captured the key components of a winning team with superior leadership and strategy operating in a Level Five culture. His stories and descriptions are written in his wonderful communicating style – funny, self-deprecating, and wonderfully honest. He's seen every level of culture; thus, it's clear he knows what he's talking about. You'll finish

We're All In with a much greater appreciation of what the characteristics of a great culture are, and how to start building yours toward Level Five. He's given us an incredibly useful book, full of "tools for your toolbox." Don't hesitate to make notes in the margins, tab key pages, and make full use of the checklists for success he includes in the last chapter. *We're All In* should be a desk-side reference for every leader, at every level, in every organization.

In the crazy world we live in today, there are few leaders who are stepping up and setting the right example, and giving us the moral compass we need to create an environment where people feel as though they belong to something greater than themselves. Major General Robert Mixon has given us that leadership in this remarkable book. I'm so glad our initial meeting has become a lifetime relationship.

Jeff Nix, Assistant General Manager, Detroit Pistons

Acknowledgments

It's hard to capture how much I owe to so many people who have shown me what a world-class culture looks like, so I'll say up front this is only a small part of those who have influenced me through the years. Like most of us, I think, we are the sum of the lives of others we have interacted with. The great news for me is that these were people of depth, sincerity, compassion, and conviction.

First among these is my spouse and best friend of over 40 years, Ruth. Everyone who knows her reports that she is the most decent person they've known, and she exemplifies the only piece of my father's guidance that I got that I followed. "Son", he said, "Make sure you marry *up*."

Our two sons, Rob and Russ, are men of character and integrity, and Ruth is a key reason they grew up that way. And when it came time for them to get some guidance from their old man about marriage, I told them same thing my father told me. And it appears they have actually listened. Ruth is the role model they wanted their life partners to be like, and that's about the greatest tribute anyone could have.

My bosses across the span of four plus decades represent a remarkable cross section from poor leaders to great, but I was fortunate to have far more of the latter than the former. From my first leader, Army Captain David M. Robinson III, to my last one, Mr. Sankar Sewnauth, each one profoundly affected my understanding of building and sustaining a culture of excellence. I am indebted to each one.

The incredibly talented and dedicated young men in the West Point Class of 1974 have also made an indelible impression on the cultural values I hold dear, and I'm honored to be a member of the "Pride of the Corps, '74." We have truly been a band of brothers in virtually every respect, and today our bonds are stronger than they were almost 50 years ago.

Finally, I am deeply indebted to the love and support of my mom, Gay, who raised all 6 of us in the midst of conditions that were often challenging and stressful. We all loved Dad, but Mom was the glue that held us together. That, too, is part of the fabric of a world-class culture. When you feel as though you belong, anything is possible. Enjoy the journey!

Introduction

One of my close friends and West Point classmates, Bill Higgs, co-founded and led a business called Mustang Engineering. In the dedication of his book telling the company's story, he wrote that one of the key components of their phenomenal success was the development of the Mustang culture: He writes, "as the history of Mustang unfolds, [we seek] to show how our concept of being caretakers rather than owners facilitated the development of a strong culture that set the organization up to overachieve."[1]

While culture is a frequently used term, it's important to understand what the word means. Culture is defined as a way of thinking, working, and behaving that exists in an organization.[2] Essentially then, culture is our organizational ecosystem. This book is about developing a world-class culture in your team, department, and organization. I call the optimum state the

---

1   *Mustang: the Story, From Zero to $1 Billion*, Bill Higgs, Haven Creative Press, 2016, p. 4.

2   Merriam Webster's Dictionary actual definition is "the set of shared attitudes, values, goals, and practices that characterizes an institution or organization."

Level 5 culture because it represents the pinnacle of an operating environment.

Why Level 5? The idea of having five levels of a culture is similar to having five levels of leadership. In my experience, there are definite stages of development in a culture, and in this book, I'll describe what those stages look like. Over the course of this book, not only will you gain a better understanding of the five levels of culture, but you will also learn how to improve your organization's behavior and performance to take your company to Level 5. In the culture of excellence Level 5 represents, leaders and teams work in harmony every day to ensure the organization is healthy, dynamic, innovative, and profitable. Everyone is "All In."

What do we mean by five levels of culture? The levels were originally developed as a descriptor for individual leadership, derived by several leaders, authors, and researchers to delineate various stages of leadership development. In my work, both in the military and the private sector, I've discovered these descriptors are relevant to team cultures as well. There are stages of growth and development for individuals, groups, and their interactive behaviors. Once we can identify these stages, we can help to reach the next growth phase.

Throughout my military and corporate career, I've learned much about these levels of cultural excellence (or in some cases, levels of cultural mediocrity) and how effective leaders can inspire real change in companies and organizations. Some of these lessons were learned the hard way, through mistakes I've witnessed or made myself. But mistakes are where the real learning occurs.

Over the course of the following chapters, I'll give you some practical tools you can start using tomorrow to take your culture from where it is today toward a Level 5 culture of excellence, and sustain it. This will be a journey, so don't expect overnight results. It can take several years to change the culture in any organization.[3] A plan of action will help you to see the journey through. And this book will help you develop that plan. Even small changes can help bring big impact, so while it may take time for your organization to truly reach Level 5, I'm certain you'll see results worth celebrating.

To achieve real change, the most important thing a leader can offer his or her team is *persistence*. Change is hard, even in the best companies. However, persistent leadership will help overcome the inevitable setbacks you'll encounter in your cultural journey to Level 5—where everyone owns the present and the future. And in getting there, your competition won't be able to touch you. If you dedicate yourself to staying the course, the results will be game changing.

---

3   There are a number of case studies indicating a timeframe of 2–3 years is fairly accurate across various types of companies and organizations, but the key point here is the fact that cultural change takes time.

Chapter 1:
What Right Looks Like

I didn't always understand what a great culture looks like. In fact, as a young West Point cadet and later as an Army officer I only had a vague notion of what a culture was at all. We had a set way of doing things, to be sure, but it was pretty much taken for granted that we all knew why we did things "the military way." Throughout my journey as a soldier, though, I came to understand that there was, indeed, a difference between healthy cultures and toxic ones. The former generated continued excellence, because we were vested in the outcome; the latter drove off many of the best and brightest, because there was no effort to make us want to buy in. The sad part was that, in many cases, the toxic cultures endured for periods of time before their hollow infrastructures began

to cave in. Many good officers and soldiers suffered when that time came.

The tipping point I experienced was in the mid-1970s in the U.S. Army in what was then West Germany. We literally encountered the perfect cultural storm—the clash of a draft Army with a new volunteer force, the widespread public disapproval of maintaining a large standing Army in the aftermath of the Vietnam defeat, the increasing popularity of drugs, and the continuing effects of racial bias. As young officers, we often witnessed riots in the barracks and illegal behaviors by soldiers. Discipline was sporadic. Our vehicles lacked spare parts and fuel for training exercises that were badly needed to sustain combat readiness. We were becoming a hollow force.

The strong measures President Reagan put into place in the early 1980s enabled the U.S. military to slowly emerge from the cultural abyss that the organization was facing, but it took years to pull ourselves out of it. Those of us that survived said later that we could have predicted the outcome—but we were slow to anticipate the need for change until it was almost too late. We had to learn the hard way.

Here's another company story of the difficulty of anticipating the need for cultural change until it was almost too late:

> In the early 2000s Aetna was struggling mightily on all fronts. While on the surface revenues remained strong, its rapport with customers and physicians was rapidly eroding, and its reputation was being bludgeoned by lawsuits and a national backlash against health maintenance organizations and managed care (which Aetna had championed). To boot, the company was losing roughly $1 million a

day, thanks to cumbersome processes and enormous overhead, as well as unwise acquisitions.

Many of the problems Aetna faced were attributed to its culture—especially its reverence for the company's 150-year history. Once openly known among workers as "Mother Aetna," the culture encouraged employees to be steadfast to the point that they'd become risk-averse, tolerant of mediocrity, and suspicious of outsiders. The prevailing executive mind-set was "We take care of our people for life, as long as they show up every day and don't cause trouble." Employees were naturally wary of any potential threat to that bargain. When Aetna merged with U.S. Healthcare, a lower-cost health care provider, in 1996, a major culture clash ensued. But instead of adapting to U.S. Healthcare's more-aggressive ways, the conservative Aetna culture only became more intransigent. Aetna's leaders could make little headway against it, and one CEO was forced out after failing to change it.

What Aetna's management didn't recognize was that you can't trade your company's culture in as if it were a used car. For all its benefits and blemishes, it's a legacy that remains uniquely yours. Unfortunately, it can feel like a millstone when a company is trying to push through a significant change—a merger, for instance, or a turnaround. Cultural inclinations are well entrenched, for good or bad. But it's possible to draw on the positive aspects of culture, turning them to your advantage, and offset some of the negative aspects as you go. This approach makes change far easier to implement.

In late 2000, John W. Rowe, MD, became Aetna's fourth CEO in five years. Employees skeptically prepared for yet another exhausting effort to transform the company into an efficient growth engine. This time, however, they were in for a surprise. Rowe didn't walk in with a new strategy and try to force a cultural shift to achieve it. Instead, right from the start, he, along with Ron Williams (who joined Aetna in 2001 and became its president in 2002), took time to visit the troops, understand their perspective, and involve them in the planning. With other members of the senior team, they sought out employees at all levels—those who were well connected, sensitive to the company culture, and widely respected—to get their input on the strategy as well as their views on both the design and execution of intended process changes.

These conversations helped Rowe and his team identify Aetna's biggest problem: A strategy that focused narrowly on managing medical expenses to reduce the cost of claims while alienating the patients and physicians that were key to Aetna's long-term success. At the same time, they surfaced Aetna's significant cultural strengths: a deep-seated concern about patients, providers, and employers; underlying pride in the history and purpose of the company; widespread respect for peers; and a large group of dedicated professionals.

These insights led Rowe to rethink his approach to the company's turnaround. He declared that instead of just cutting costs, the organization would pursue a strategy he called "the New Aetna." It would build a winning position in health insurance and a strong

4

brand by attracting and serving both patients and health care providers well. That was an appealing proposition but would require significant restructuring; no one's job was guaranteed. In other words, it was the kind of change that Mother Aetna traditionally resisted with every passive-aggressive move she could muster. But this time, without ever describing their efforts as "cultural change," top management began with a few interventions. These interventions led to small but significant behavioral changes that, in turn, revitalized Aetna's culture while preserving and championing its strengths.

For instance, the New Aetna was specifically designed to reinforce employees' commitment to customers—reflected in the firm's history of responding quickly to natural disasters. Rowe also made a point of reinforcing a longtime strength that had eroded—employees' pride in the company. When, in an off-the-cuff response to a question at a town hall meeting, he highlighted pride as a reason employees should get behind change, he received a spontaneous standing ovation. So while the plan for change challenged long-held assumptions (among other things, it would require the elimination of 5,000 jobs, with more cuts likely to come), it was embraced by employees. They had been heard and appreciated, and they came to accept the New Aetna.

Indeed, during the next few years it became clear, from surveys, conversations, and observation, that a majority of Aetna's employees felt reinvigorated, enthusiastic, and genuinely proud of the company. And Aetna's financial performance reflected that. By the mid-2000s, the company was earning close to $5 million a day. Its operating income recovered from a $300 million loss to a $1.7 billion gain. From May 2001 to January 2006, its stock price rose steadily, from $5.84 (split adjusted) to $48.40 a share.[4]

The New Aetna story is one where visionary, persistent leadership enabled true cultural change across a large, complex organization. The campaign required leadership and persistence, but the results were enduring. The New Aetna became a positive ecosystem where people valued their roles and responsibilities in the organization; they nurtured a deep appreciation for the company's mission, intent (end state, key tasks, and purpose), values, and culture because they recognized the benefits for each of them individually. Clearly, many of the best and brightest chose to be part of the New Aetna, despite the uncertainty of change which they knew would result in some employees losing their jobs. They wanted to keep the pride and customer focus of Mother Aetna, and John Rowe and his key leaders were smart enough to see that. It was important to retain the goodness of the old culture as they built the new one.

What are key ingredients in the development of a world-class culture like the one the New Aetna represents? The journey to developing this Level 5 culture is rooted in *bringing the right values to life*—values like integrity, trust, and transparency. It also includes *modeling behaviors* where leaders share credit for accomplishments, while accepting responsibility for failures.

There is a strong sense of belonging in the culture of excellence. For example, Google found that the best teams created a culture

---

4   Excerpt from the article "Cultural Change That Sticks" by Jon R. Katzenbach, Ilona Steffen, and Caroline Kronley in the July–August 2012 issue of *Harvard Business Review*

of "psychological safety," meaning team members could share information and thoughts freely without fear of retribution.[5] In this culture, mistakes don't get passed around the organization. No one plays the "blame game." Instead, Level 5 leaders and teams model *mutual* accountability. The boss doesn't have to chew anyone's posterior, because peers chew each other's posteriors when something doesn't get done or doesn't meet the standard.

The development of strong mutual accountability is one of the most significant stages of cultural development. Dave Logan, John King, and Halee Fischer-Wright describe the stages of accountability and explain how we, as people, are essentially tribal in their book, *Tribal Leadership*.[6] The authors developed the book as the result of a 10-year study which examined the qualities and characteristics of 24,000 people and two dozen companies. The research led them to conclude that tribal cultures evolve through several stages.

The journey follows individual members and their processes of integrating into the culture. The evolution begins with stage one, where a person feels that "All life sucks." In stage two, the person recognizes "My individual life sucks." During stage three, the person thinks that "I'm great and others are not." Beginning with stage four, the person recognizes that "We're great." Finally, in stage five, "Life is great." Over the course of the evolution of a successful, healthy culture, the tribe's well-being becomes more important than that of the individual

---

5   "In Search of a Perfect Team," by Stu Woo, *The Wall Street Journal*, Monday, March 13, 2017, p. R6.

6   *Tribal Leadership: Leveraging Natural Groups to Build a Thriving Organization* by Dave Logan, John King, and Halee Fischer-Wright, Harper-Collins 2008.

members. Mutual accountability is the most important aspect of accountability in stage five.

In the United States Army, culture is built around the concept of "Be-Know-Do."[7] This framework builds on some of the aspects of tribal behavior by bringing a new recruit immediately into stage four of the Logan, King, and Fischer-Wright model. Through the boot camp process, a new military recruit will soon know life sucks on an individual level and he will suffer personal hardship, fear, and self-doubt. However, he soon learns to accept the premise that "We're great and life is great" because now he or she can belong to something bigger than they are. The military mantra of *Mission First, People Always* becomes the soldier's way of life. Soldiers don't want to let their comrades down. Every day they learn to live the concept of mutual accountability.

The Army's cultural model, which focuses on what the authors of *Tribal Leadership* call stages four and five of cultural evolution, is an excellent descriptor of how to rapidly assimilate individuals into a high performing "All In" organization. This book will help translate this concept from military to corporate life, and give you a set of practical tools to help you determine where your organization is now, where it's going (or where you want it to go), and how to get there. This is not just a case of translating Army culture into corporate culture. Rather, we are examining how to adopt the best practices of the Army's Be-Know-Do model into a viable corporate ecosystem. The Level 5 culture of excellence represents all of the qualities where people feel

---

7   An excellent description of the Army's cultural model is presented in the book *"Be-Know-Do" Leadership the Army Way* by the Leader to Leader Institute, Jossey-Bass, 2004, with a foreword by Francis Hesselbein and General (retired) Eric K, Shinseki.

as though they *belong*—along with the dynamic, healthy environment which nurtures and protects it.

What's in it for us as corporate leaders to build and nurture a Level 5 culture? Clearly, it's bottom line results and industry leadership. The most successful companies in the world today invest in having a world-class culture. Think of Disney, Google, Southwest Airlines, Adobe...the list is substantial. These companies invest in their cultures, cultivate them, protect them. It is their corporate edge, delighting shareholders, to be sure, but also helping to establish themselves as leaders in their industry.

On the flip side, we've all seen the dark outcomes where cultures have been allowed to languish in mediocrity. The recent debacle in United Airlines, in which a passenger was forcibly removed from a flight to allow crew members to travel, underscores how toxic a major company culture can become. With the increasing amount of information available to employees at every level, the lack of customer focus and employee loyalty by the senior management can become viral in a matter of hours or days. Culture defines us today.

Chapter 2:
Level 5 Leaders Don't Automatically Create Level 5 Cultures

In my series of blogs, I've described the importance of developing Level Five leaders in your organization.[8] However, there's an important distinction between Level 5 leadership and Level 5 culture. Just because you have a corps of strong individual leaders, it does not mean that they are going to automatically create a Level 5 culture.

The reality is more complicated, because there can be real tension among even the best leaders. Great leaders don't always perform well in teams, despite possessing all of the qualities and characteristics associated with dedicated, focused leadership.[9]

---

8   Two of the most prominent authors on the concept of Level Five leadership are Jim Collins and John C. Maxwell, who wrote two books on the subject: *Good to Great* (Collins) and *Level 5 Leadership* (Maxwell). See their definitions of Level Five leaders for a good comparative description of each level, and evidence of their research on this topic, as well as our blogs and articles on the subject.

9   The best book I have seen thus far in describing this tension among high performers when put together on teams is Patrick Lencioni's *The Five Dysfunctions of a Team: A Leadership Fable*, San Francisco, Jossey-Bass, 2002.

A leader may be dynamic, energetic, and overachieving. But two or more leaders may not focus that energy in the same direction. One of the biggest challenges to teams is establishing cooperation among leaders, which is essential to harnessing their collective energy and talent, for the good of the organization.

It's hard to overstate the importance of building high performing teams if you're going to grow your organization into a Level 5 culture. The realities of the world in which we live dictate that we must learn to adapt quickly and continuously.

What's changed? I used to think that we were living in a world where there were very few totally new ideas. In fact, I had narrowed our species' truly revolutionary ideas down to two: fire and the wheel. Now I'm convinced that I must add one more: the Internet. We are living in a time of revolutionary change, spurred on by the information age. Our world has become far more complex in a matter of just a few years.

Perhaps one of the best books about this transformation is General (retired) Stan McChrystal's *Team of Teams*.[10] The book is a detailed analysis of how the world has changed and how we must adapt to this new environment, told through the lens of McChrystal's experience in the Special Operations Task Force in Iraq. Of his time fighting Al Qaeda during a particularly vicious insurgency that emerged after the U.S. invasion toppled Saddam Hussein's regime, McChrystal writes:

> In October 2003, just after I took command of the Task Force, I inspected the intelligence facilities at our small base at Baghdad International Airport (BIAP). The term 'Intelligence facilities' paints a

---

10   *Team of Teams: New Rules of Engagement for a Complex World.* General Stanley McChrystal (USA retired), Tantum Collins, David Silverman, and Chris Fussell. New York: Penguin Random House LLC, 2015.

more impressive picture than the reality. Housed in a small building were cells for the temporary confinement of detainees captured on task force raids, an interrogation room, and a decrepit office area. As I walked around asking questions and getting a sense of the operation, I opened the door to a supply closet. Inside was a four foot high mound of plastic bags and burlap sacks—evidence that our forward teams had been flying back. The bags were all piled up, unopened.

It turned out that when one of our forward-operating SEAL or Army Special Forces teams captured intelligence documents during a raid, they tossed everything—documents, CDs, computers, cell phones—into sandbags, trash bags, or whatever they had, typically tying a tag or affixing a Post-it note of explanation. Then they would throw those bags onto choppers returning to Baghdad, alongside mail, un-needed equipment, or even important detainees. The bags would not arrive for hours, and the scribbled Post-its, many of which got lost along the way, never provided sufficient context for the rear-operating [intelligence] to do its job.

The supervisor of the facility explained that, lacking dedicated translators, he used the interrogators' translators during their spare time, and there wasn't much spare time. Like ripe fruit left in the sun, intelligence spoils quickly. By the time the bags were opened, most of it was worthless…a map to Saddam Hussein's hiding spot could have lain among the documents and we wouldn't have known.

The operators, adept at their own roles but having little understanding of the nuts and bolts of intel analysis, could not anticipate what sorts of explanations would be meaningful, what sort of context was relevant, or what material could be turned around instantly and which could wait...

On the intel side, analysts were frustrated by the poor quality of materials and the delays in receiving them...to them, every cell phone or dirty piece of paper they received was just another assignment handed down by a manager...

The teams were operating independently—like workers in an efficient factory—while trying to keep pace with an interdependent environment. ... The unopened bags of evidence were symptomatic of a larger problem. ... The choke point existed not because of insufficient guidance from above, but because of a dearth of integration.

To fix the choke point, we needed to fix the management system and organizational culture that created it. As soon as we looked at the organization through the lens of the team structure—for weaknesses in horizontal connectivity rather than new possibilities for top-down planning—similar choke points became visible between all our individual teams.[11]

General McChrystal's realization that he had a superb war-fighting set of teams that was organized for the last war, not the one they were in, led him to uncover the notion that *complexity* had replaced *complicated* in team dynamics. "Being *complex*

---

11   Ibid., pp. 120–122.

is different than being *complicated*," McChrystal writes, "The workings of a complicated device like an internal combustion engine might be confusing, but they can ultimately be broken down into a neat and tidy set of deterministic relationships... Complexity, on the other hand, occurs when the number of *interactions* increases dramatically—the interdependencies that allow bank viruses and bank runs to spread; this is where things become unpredictable. ... The density of interactions means that even a relatively small number of elements can quickly defy prediction."[12]

To further compound the challenge of complexity that the information age has created across cultures, there are inherent frictions at work in teams. Otherwise highly capable and successful leaders can find the process of building and leading teams to be confusing, disruptive, and frustrating. Patrick Lencioni captured the dysfunctions of a team in describing the challenges leaders and other high performers must overcome when organized into teams:

1. Absence of Trust

2. Fear of Conflict

3. Lack of Commitment

4. Avoidance of Accountability

5. Inattention to Results

Effectively overcoming these dysfunctions is fundamental in building a Level 5 culture. Each of the five tendencies must be deliberately addressed or the team will fail—or at the very least, seriously underperform.

---

12 Ibid., p. 57.

Teamwork and cooperation don't come naturally; we have to work at it. Think about that. As kids, what was one of the first things our parents tried to teach us? They taught us to cooperate with others, to share, to play nice. Just as leaders are made rather than born, cultures of excellence where strong teamwork exists are also made, not born. Creating this "we" culture is one of the critical tasks great leaders have to learn to nurture in a very deliberate way.

Good leaders are ambitious, energetic and caring. But, in order to become *great* leaders, they need to exemplify the qualities of persistence and humility in the board room so others want to do the same. Level 5 cultures consist of people sincerely focused on the good of the organization above their personal benefit. They understand and accept the fact that the organization's success will, in many ways, create their own sense of well-being and success.

What is the role of leaders and what do they contribute to creating a culture of excellence? Level 5 leaders have to incorporate the Army's principles of *"Be–Know–Do"* by deliberately influencing the thinking, behaving, and working of the people in the organization. They have to repeat the mission frequently, establish and model the leader's intent (more about the concept of intent later), and drive the organization to operate within these parameters. The Level 5 leadership establishes a set of shared values that are repeated often. They also define expected behaviors in writing. And they commit to training high performing teams.

One person who embodies the leadership qualities of growing high performing teams that contribute to developing a Level 5 culture is General (retired) Colin Powell. I had the privilege to serve on his personal staff when he was the Chairman of the Joint Chiefs of Staff. I observed him radiate the qualities that help to create a Level 5 culture. He was unquestionably the leader of the organization, in addition to being one of the leaders of the United States. However, when he talked to someone, his focus and presence made him or her feel as though s/he were the only person in the room. General Powell understood the critical importance of building and leading integrated teams in creating a culture of excellence:

> Every good leader I have known understands instinctively the need to communicate to followers a common purpose, a purpose that comes down from the leader and is internalized by the entire team. Armed with a common purpose, an organization's various parts will strive to achieve that purpose and will not go riding off in every direction.
>
> I have also seen many organizations that resemble nothing less than warring tribes. They usually fail.[13]

General Powell insisted on cooperation and shared values among the 1500 members of the Joint Staff, which was largely made up of senior officers of all the military services as well as senior civilian executives. Big egos didn't last long on his team of teams. He clearly understood the importance setting individual egos aside.

Effective, disciplined team leadership is thus a core element of building a Level 5 culture. Great leaders have to be deliberate in establishing the environment where "we" replaces "I" in the way people think and behave, every day. They must see beyond themselves.

---

13 *It Worked for Me in Life and Leadership,* General (retired) Colin Powell with Tony Koltz. New York: Harper Collins, 2012, p. 207.

Chapter 3:
Seeing Yourself

So when we say "Great leaders must see beyond themselves," what exactly does that mean? To see where you stand in terms of your culture, take this brief quiz below. Your answers will help to determine where you are and give you an idea of some of the cultural challenges you may be up against.

Question 1

Do people normally make eye contact in your workplace? Although this is a relatively Western phenomenon, in our part of the world we consider it a mark of confidence and pride when people make eye contact when passing or conversing with one another.

Question 2

Do people smile? I think we all know what genuine smiles are—those where people seem sincerely pleased. These are the smiles I'm talking about, versus the ones which are perfunctory or contrived.

Question 3

> Are your meetings effective or ineffective? We'll discuss these definitions in more detail in succeeding paragraphs.

After answering those questions, you might be thinking: "Well, this seems like a simple process with a simple problem and a simple solution. All I have to do is make eye contact, smile, and fix my meetings." However, growing your current culture into a Level 5 culture is much harder than that. If it were easy, anybody could do it. The real challenge is in seeing yourself and how you contribute to your culture, and then identifying and implementing the tools you'll learn here to get to the Level 5 culture of "We're All In."

Organizations rarely take a linear path to excellence. Instead, the journey typically will have any number of curves, choke points, and dangerous intersections. As the leader, you must be adaptive to be successful, and bring the company back on course when faced with these obstacles. In the end, every activity and individual goal should align with the organization's true mission.

What do most of us do every day? "We spend most of the work day putting out fires," many leaders say. And that's the reality. In a world of constant change and increasing demands, uncertainty is the new certainty. We're trapped in a burning building of crises. No wonder many good people leave otherwise good organizations and teams. They don't want to be firefighters—that's for the professionals who literally do it.

One day a few years ago, when I was busy beating back the flames at work, I mentioned how hard this putting out fires stuff was to my boss. "Well," he replied, "you're not getting paid to put out fires. As a leader, you're getting paid to *prevent* them." This was a defining moment for me as a leader. I realized that I had to be more than a fire fighter. I had to become a fire prevention specialist. This was new thinking for me. It caused me to change some of my behaviors, such as reflecting nightly about what I had accomplished (or not accomplished) that day and what I needed to do to better prepare for the next day. I had to become much more of a proactive leader than a reactive one.

Like organizations, most people don't take a linear path in their individual journey to develop their personal and professional behaviors to a Level 5 standard. Make no mistake about it: You can't separate your personal conduct from your professional conduct. You can't be Dr. Jekyll and Mr. Hyde, switching between work and home. One of you is not authentic. And in the information age, there is no place to hide. The same is true of cultures. You can't have one culture in an organization in the C-Suite, and another on the front lines. As one of my colleagues in the manufacturing industry used to say, "Your culture is defined on the night shift." Your culture is demonstrated by the behaviors of your most junior team members (those are typically employed on the night shift in a manufacturing company because that's the least popular time to work).

Let's start by looking at the way people make eye contact.

Eye contact is indicative of your sense of self-worth and the sense that you're moving with a purpose. When you're looking people in the eye, you have your head up and your posture is probably better as a result. You're also much more likely to be focused and thinking about what you're doing. You're engaged in the world around you. Although it seems very simple and subtle, it indicates a lot of other positive things in your personal behavior and in your interest in other people. Something that you can immediately notice while walking around an organization is whether people are routinely looking around at each other and their surroundings.

The second question asked about smiling, which is also a key indicator of your culture's health. People who always take a negative view—the "glass half-empty crowd"—are more likely to think that yelling is a good way to get somebody's attention or motivate them. Back in the day, many leaders believed that being overtly tough and intimidating by yelling at people would get them to change their behaviors or become motivated. However, today we know better. The truth is that yelling doesn't work. Even in the military, a place once known for the cliché of a shouting drill sergeant, yelling has been discounted as a methodology.

The whole idea of having a positive outlook, seeing the glass as half-full, transcends many other aspects of growing your culture to the next level. If you take your work very seriously but not yourself, you can have that self-deprecating way of smiling and having fun.

"We enjoy what we're doing and we're going to have fun." You can even state that as part of your culture. Many great companies pride themselves on having cultures where team members enjoy what they're doing and enjoy being around one another. These are organizations where you don't have to look far to find a smile. Just like eye contact, smiling is an indicator that a lot of other good things are going on in your organization.

The third question helps identify what I call Low Value Meetings. These meetings are also indicators for a number of negative factors in your current culture. Low Value Meetings are caused by people not valuing one another's time. They believe that if they can get everybody together in some forum like a room, then they'll be more productive than they would be if they were operating separately. There's no real evidence to substantiate that belief. In fact, my experience observing and participating in meeting-heavy organizations is that most of the time spent in meetings is wasted, particularly when these Low Value Meetings occur back-to-back.

I know many executives who live in this meeting environment, and they freely admit it's a source of constant frustration. It's almost impossible to go into consecutive meetings well-informed or come out of them with useful takeaways and outcomes. Following up is nearly impossible. Usually Low Value Meetings point to low attendee morale. They're not going to be smiling and making a lot of eye contact, because they're not having fun and they don't feel appreciated. They believe meetings are just a grind. LVMs are a serious drain on morale, and they stifle cultural growth and creativity. As Patty McCord, former Chief Talent Officer at Netflix, describes it:

"When I advise leaders about molding a corporate culture, I tend to see three issues that need attention. This type of mismatch is one… I often sit in on company meetings to get a sense of how people operate. I frequently see CEOs who are clearly winging it. They lack a real agenda. They're working from slides that were obviously put together an hour before or were recycled from the previous round of…meetings.

Workers notice these things, and if they see a leader who's not fully prepared and who relies on charm, IQ, and improvisation, it affects how they perform, too. It's a waste of time to articulate ideas about values and culture if you don't model and reward behavior that aligns with those goals."[14]

LVMs usually lack structure. They often have no clear agenda, nobody keeps a record of the discussion (or even take notes), and there's no published set of deliverables at the end which outline who will do what by when. If this describes your meetings, then you have a serious culture problem. Messy, disorganized meetings are a key indicator that people don't feel that their leaders view their time as valuable and are willing to waste it.

Many Low Value Meeting conversations consist of one person briefing his or her statistics or data to the leader of the group. While this is happening, everyone else in the room isn't paying attention because they're either preparing to give their report or they've mentally checked out after having their turn. Think about your experiences. How many times do you remember a recent meeting? Most of us have no recollection of them beyond a couple of hours after they've ended. We've moved on. And that's because we were not invested in the meetings in the first place. When we believe we have little value in being part of the meeting audience in the first place, and we spend most of the session just sitting there, it's no wonder the event is forgettable.

To make matters worse, in Low Value Meetings, the leader usually speaks first. When the leader speaks first, any healthy discussion or differing views about how to address an issue are now much less likely to surface. Unfortunately, everybody else in the room is less inclined to differ with his opinion.

---

14 "How Netflix Reinvented HR" by Patty McCord in the *Harvard Business Review*, January-February 2014, p. 4.

Instead, they're going to reply something along the lines of, "Great idea Boss!"—even though they may have a much better, more productive idea. They're going to be too intimidated to come forward. At best, no one wants to rock the boat.

Leaders of High Value Meetings take a completely different approach. Contrary to the Low Value Meeting, which can be a full room of the wrong strategic participants, the best meetings are held one-on-one. This is when you can read the body language, listen to the tone, and sense what's really being said. They take more time than group meetings, but this is time well spent. And, there are also times when larger meetings make sense. In these sessions in a Level 5 culture, the leader speaks *last*, yielding the floor to his subordinates so they can make their opinions known without fear of contradicting the boss. High Value Meetings are structured to not waste time. They have a published agenda. They have specific topics that will be discussed and decisions that will be made. High Value Meetings have outcomes and deliverables where attendees are assigned tasks and the participants are able to report on their progress at the next meeting to show how much closer they are to reaching a goal. The best meetings aren't scheduled right before or after other meetings, so participants have time to prepare beforehand and to process the information afterward.

Tools for Effective Meetings

- Have an agenda

- Send out the agenda in advance of the meeting

- Designate someone to chair the meeting

- Designate someone to take minutes

- Have a time limit

- Reserve a location

- Make arrangements for any A/V equipment if needed

- Make sure to invite all who should attend (and not those who shouldn't)

- Have a plan to move on to the next item if discussion gets stalled

- Send out minutes afterward with actions and responsible parties

- Use the 4 Agreements:[15]

  · Be impeccable with your word

  · Don't take anything personally

  · Don't make assumptions

  · Always do your best

Three simple questions have answers that can tell you a lot about where you are on your cultural journey. If you are honest in your answers, you'll probably see there is considerable room for improvement in at least one area, if not all three. The real question is whether you'll take action to establish the environment where people make eye contact, smile, and focus on High Value Meetings.

---

15 *The Four Agreements* by Don Miguel Ruiz. San Rafael: Amber Allen Publishing, 1997. Dr. Ruiz has a superb set of guidelines for professional conduct.

Chapter 4:
The Importance of Having the Right Culture

West Point and the U.S. military underwent some significant changes as part of a cultural transformation during the 1980s and 1990s. This cultural transformation was prompted by several factors, including a rapidly-changing global environment. Chief among the concerns at West Point in those days was that there was a very strong chance that the academy might lose its relevancy unless it changed its culture. At the time, attrition rates were extremely high. During the 1970s—when I was enrolled—the attrition rate was upwards of 40%. To understand the magnitude of this problem, you need to understand that the process begins with screening roughly 10,000 applicants—a huge investment—and, from that pool, the selection of around 1,400 applicants to be cadets. Typically, 40% of the cadets would subsequently leave prior to graduation, either voluntarily or involuntarily—a significant waste of our national resources.

In the 1980s, West Point's more visionary leaders realized that their culture was in danger. Something had to change; the organizational culture had to evolve. This cultural transformation meant moving away from promoting values like compliance and instead moving toward empowerment. In many ways, it represented a tectonic shift for this venerable institution with a 200-year legacy. Changing the culture would be a long, arduous process, even when most agree (which is questionable in this case, with the tremendous pressure of tradition). Under ideal conditions, it takes two to three years to change a culture. At West Point, it would take much longer.

One of the most powerful factors at work to accelerate this change, though, was the acceptance of females into the Corps of Cadets, which began in 1976. Challenging one of the world's most established male bastions, females had to adapt to a harsh, biased environment. My first experience with this fundamental change occurred in 1982, when I joined the faculty of the Department of History at West Point. It was immediately clear to me as I stood in front of 15 cadets in the classroom that a significant cultural shift was underway. You could almost feel the tension in the air.

Now the forces of cultural change were under even greater pressure to move in the direction of more commitment, higher buy-in from the cadets, the faculty, and the Army. There were tangible changes in behaviors being implemented in the 1980s— the cadets could eat more, sleep a little more, and endure less verbal abuse. But the academic, physical, and military requirements remained strict. West Point remained a daunting challenge for every cadet who stepped inside the gate, regardless of gender. The pivotal factor would be whether the Corps of Cadets would successfully adapt its culture.

Yet, this would prove to be a significant transformation and one that has greatly benefited the Army as a whole. To give you some idea of the success of this change, my son's West Point class (2011) had *half* the attrition rate experienced by my class

(1974).[16] This decline in attrition brought West Point to a rate on par with most of the leading four-year colleges and universities in the nation, which average an 82% graduation rate. It is a direct result of having created the right culture at the right time. And it's a testimony to the courage of the leadership who sustained their commitment in the face of enormous resistance to change.

Building the right culture demands focusing on the future, growing leaders who learn to think ahead and anticipate what needs to be done…and to do it. Unfortunately, this idea can often offend insecure leaders. The best leaders are servant leaders. They live vicariously through the success of those they are privileged to lead. It means accepting and embracing the fact that bringing out the best in others is our primary responsibility.

Leaders in a Level 5 culture put a lot of effort into giving feedback, and carefully assessing team member performance *and* potential. In fact, one of the key activities in the Level 5 culture is a deliberate talent planning process. Not only does this process ensure team members receive consistent, meaningful feedback, but also that the leadership is committed to developing a career path for individuals. The best culture is one where leaders invest in each other; to help individuals have every opportunity to reach their full potential.

People want to feel they contribute to the greater good. Not long ago, I heard a powerful story that illustrates this concept. A car dealer told me about a chance encounter he had at the end of a workday with one of his service technicians. The technician

---

16   My West Point class suffered approximately 40% attrition over the period 1 July 1970 to 5 June 1974. According to the 2012 report to the West Point Board of Visitors by the Admissions Department, "Over the past 30 years our graduation rates climbed and then remained steady at approximately 80%."

was just finishing up a repair when the dealer approached and asked him what he had accomplished that day. The service technician replied, "Well, today I made nine families' lives safer."

Note the technician's words. He didn't simply say, "I fixed nine cars." Instead, he was looking at the bigger picture and saw how his repairs would help drivers and their families be far safer. The technician viewed his work as being more than just a job. He had bought into his company's culture and recognized the value of his work. He was "All In."

Surveys conducted in companies and organizations throughout the country indicate that only about 13% of people in the workforce are really "All In."[17] The term deserves some explanation at this point. When we say we're "All In" that means we are fully committed to the goals of the organization; we have aligned our personal values to the company's values.

This means that the remaining 87% are somewhere in the middle—or they're out on the far end. Some of that can be assessed and developed in the talent planning process. However, it serves as an indication as to where you are in terms of growing the next level of leaders and having a goal to continuously get better. Culture is never static; it either gets better or gets worse.

West Point's development of a more empowering culture is a great example of how even the most established institutions can develop leaders who effectively see themselves and their environment, recognize when the dots aren't connecting anymore, and take action to develop the right culture at the right time.

---

17 This statistic comes from the *Gallup* article, "Worldwide, 13% of Employees are Engaged at Work" by Steve Crabtree, October 8, 2013.

Chapter 5:
Applying the Big 6™ to Your Culture

So far, we've talked about what right looks like in terms of culture, the importance of seeing yourself, and the value of developing the right culture at the right time. One of the key ingredients in developing a Level 5 culture with these attributes is the application of our Big 6™ Leadership Principles. These key principles were developed over a lifetime of trial and error. I've seen them employed effectively in organizations large and small with remarkable effect. These principles help you grow leaders who get it and who set the conditions for a healthy, productive work environment. The Big 6™ principles are:

- Set the Azimuth

- Listen

- Trust and Empower

- Do the Right Thing When No One is Looking

- When in Charge, Take Charge

- Balance the Personal and Professional

We'll discuss the application of each of these principles through-out the rest of this chapter.

Principle 1: Set the Azimuth

Let's start with setting the azimuth. When you set your azimuth, you establish the cardinal direction for your organization. Traditionally, soldiers navigated using a map and a lensatic compass (prior to the advent of satellites and GPS). We would literally "shoot an azimuth" with our compass from where we were on the ground to another visible point on our map,

and then follow the direction of the azimuth until we got to that point, then shoot another one. So we would find our way from one location to another using a series of these waypoints.

In the corporate world, we now use azimuth in a little broader context: Your mission, intent, values, and culture are all captured in writing as your company's "azimuth." It's important that you don't just have a strategic planning session or senior executive meeting where you hammer out these ideas only to put them on the shelf never to be seen again. These are living documents which your leaders need to revisit on a regular basis, and they serve as the engine of your organization.

The mission is the who, what, and why of your organization, which can usually be summed up in one or two sentences. "Who are we? What do we do? Why do we do it?" When you write the mission as a leadership team, it's not directed or driven by one person or one leader. As you determine your mission, you start to align your organization, and that alignment is a powerful component of a Level 5 culture. Here are some examples of effective mission statements:[18]

Level Five Associates Mission

Level Five Associates provides values-based leadership development, coaching, and strategic planning to build and sustain cultures of excellence.

PepsiCo Mission

PepsiCo is one of the largest food and beverage companies in the world. We provide consumers around the world with delicious, affordable, convenient and complementary food and beverages. We are committed to investing in our people, our company and the communities where we operate to help position the company for long-term, sustainable growth.

7-Eleven Mission

At 7-Eleven, our purpose and mission is to make life a little easier for our guests by being where they need us, whenever they need us. From sales associates

---

18 The 3 mission statements are derived from the web sites of each company where they are posted.

to franchisees and managers, from fresh-sandwich makers to doughnut bakers, from daily-delivery drivers to department heads—all of us associated with 7-Eleven are here to ensure that we meet our store guests' needs with fast, convenient and friendly service and the products they want while on the go."

Without the alignment of your azimuth, all you have is a collection of individuals who are more concerned with their individual or department agendas than the good of the organization. And, your people are most likely siloed, focusing primarily on their own work, in their departments, teams, and divisions.

The leader's intent is the more definitive scope of your mission. The intent has 3 components: The first component is your desired end state, typically in a three- to five-year horizon. Ask yourself what you want to achieve and what you want your company to look like in the next three to five years.

Next, the intent lists the key tasks that must be accomplished to reach that end state. Finally, the purpose for each key task becomes the "why." As author Simon Sinek notes, the "why" is important—and not just to millennials.[19]

We learned the concept of the leader's intent from the military. Also known as the commander's intent, it was initially developed during the Napoleonic Wars of the early 19th century. During one crucial battle, one of Napoleon's marshals (senior commanders) saved the day for the French Army by arriving on the battlefield just when they were about to be overrun by the enemy. Afterward, Napoleon asked his marshal why he came

---

19 Simon Sinek is an established author and speaker, with several books published including *Start with Why* where he examines questions such as the purpose, cause, or belief that inspires you to do what you do.

to the rescue and the general answered, "Well, sir, I followed your intent. I marched to the sound of the guns."[20]

Following is an example of a more modern intent statement, derived from several actual companies. Notice there is an end state, a purpose, and the key tasks necessary to achieve that end state.

Sample Intent Statement

Purpose

Understand every customer. Provide everyone we serve with a world-class experience through our knowledge, dedication, and commitment to excellence.

Key Tasks

- Recruit, hire, grow, and retain the best people in the industry.

- Fully understand expectations, then meet or exceed them.

- Provide exceptional value and make each customer profitable for us.

- Develop and protect our culture of commitment.

- Deliver quality and price accordingly.

Desired End-State

We are the dominant provider of our products and services in the industry, with a recognized reputation for excellence.

---

20 Napoleon's marshal (General) Joachim Murat is largely credited with being the leader who originated this phrase after he saved the French Army at the battle of Eylau. Napoleon then made this a standing order to his commanders, and later one of his Generals' (Marshall Emmanuel de Grouchy) refusal to obey that order in 1815 probably contributed to the French defeat at Waterloo.

Setting the azimuth also includes establishing your values. Your values are the ethical foundation of who you are as an organization. And they can be evil as well as honorable. Adolf Hitler had values; they were just the wrong ones. The right values should embody key principles such as integrity, honesty, and loyalty. It's important to capture them in writing, build them as a team, repeat and revisit them regularly.

PepsiCo Values

- Care for our customers and the world we live in.

- Sell only products we can be proud of.

- Win with diversity and engagement.

- Balance short-term and long-term.

Finally, you want to codify the culture itself by capturing and writing out the behaviors that represent your values. You don't have to have a huge list, but you do need to codify behaviors you expect people to demonstrate every day.

Here's the culture developed by 7-Eleven:

> *Our Servant Leadership Culture Helps Us Realize Our Vision and Achieve Our Daily Mission*
>
> Our culture encourages us to work as a team, recognize outstanding performance, do our best and be accountable to each other. We are committed to serving our guests, our co-workers and the communities in which we operate.
>
> We would not be who we are without sales associates, store managers, franchisees and employees in the field and at our corporate headquarters/store support

center who work every day to offer our guests "convenience without compromise."[21]

Capturing your mission, intent, and values and then codifying your culture is a deliberate process that helps you set the azimuth—the cardinal direction—of your culture. But you have to repeat it often; keep in mind the "seven times" rule—although, in some cases, your team may need to be told seventy times! Given the importance to the direction of your company, you will need to revisit your azimuth regularly, whether it's during every key meeting or every time you're talking with your leadership team. If you bring them out repeatedly, they'll begin to come to life. Establishing the conditions for a Level 5 culture includes the continuing focus on setting and sustaining your azimuth.

Principle 2: Listen

The next principle that will pay big benefits on your journey towards a Level 5 culture is better listening. It is arguably the most difficult leadership skill to master, for a number of reasons. First, we're often not taught to listen (except for my mother, who tried in vain to convince me "God gave you two ears and one mouth for a reason..."). Second, it's not sexy to listen—it seems much more impressive to be eloquent. Third, we don't codify the benefits of effective listening. Typically, companies don't measure the costs of re-dos because the instructions weren't clearly understood the first time.

Listening has several dimensions. We must be able to listen to an individual, listen to your team (whether it's a section, crew, or department), and listen across the enterprise. Level 5

---

21   From the web site for 7-Eleven.

cultures are characterized by leaders who practice these levels of listening continuously.

Stephen Covey once famously asked, "Are you listening or just waiting to speak?"[22] I spent most of my career doing the latter, and the Army seemingly magnified that weakness by placing a large degree of emphasis on how we transmitted messages, with much less focus on how well we received them. However, we gradually developed better listening skills throughout the organization and, as we began to apply them, our culture changed.

One of those key listening skills we learned was the *backbrief.* After we received instructions for a particular task, we would then be asked by our commander to come back and say, "Sir, this is what I think you told me to do." You can conduct backbriefs individually, across departments, or across the organization. But the key element here is to focus on the listening aspect of communication rather than just the transmitting component.

Effective listening includes effective body language. In fact, the verbal component of communication is only a fraction of productive conversations.[23] Level 5 cultures are made up of leaders who practice personal communication techniques such as eye contact, cell phone discipline (face down and sound off), square up face-to-face, and taking notes. The best listeners don't stay behind a desk. They turn the computer screen away, then get up and go to a small table where they sit facing each other. Using these and the other tools tells others: "I'm getting ready to actually listen to what you have to say."

---

22 Stephen Covey is the author of *The 7 Habits of Highly Effective People* and a number other works on self-fulfillment and leadership.

23 According to most research I have uncovered, over 50% of effective communication is body language, over 30% is tone, and less than 10% is words.

These tools and techniques seem obvious, yet, they are not commonly practiced, which is why people typically don't feel as though they're being heard. I think Henry David Thoreau said it best when he observed, "The greatest compliment that was ever paid me was when one asked me what I thought, and then attended to my answer."[24]

Part of our listening challenge is brought on by the poor quality of the questions we ask. Most of us aren't good at asking questions. All too often, you'll hear questions like, "Well, how's it going?" or "How are you doing?" You won't get good information from those kinds of questions. Instead, all you'll get in response are simple answers like, "Okay," "All right," "I'm fine," or even a, "Whatever." In short, if you don't ask an informative question then you shouldn't expect an informative response. Conversely, if you deliberately construct a meaningful question, you have a good chance of getting a meaningful answer.

An example of a useful question is: "What's the biggest challenge you're facing today?" or, "What do you think is the most important thing we could do this week that would make us a better organization?" These kinds of questions are going to generate information you can use. Question architecture is important. You have to construct and practice your questions so you get useful information. Level 5 leaders build and use effective questions.

Principle 3: Trust and Empower

Our third principle is "Trust and Empower." A Level 5 culture is characterized by mutual trust and empowerment. Empowerment can be seen as the embodiment of trust, as you're putting

---

24 Thoreau as quoted in Goodreads quotes, page 1.

your faith in others and are confident in their ability to make the right decisions. These actions crystallize as the individuals embrace your trust in them.

How do you empower your team members? One tool for your toolbox is the Decision Tree. Basically, it's a tree diagram in the shape of a pyramid which outlines who makes what decisions at each level. And you guessed it, most tactical decisions are made by the people who are closest to the action. The fewest, and most strategic, are made by the senior executives.

When you build your Decision Tree, make sure you do it as a team. Let everyone else have input before you give your views or insights. Once you get the Decision Tree up, bring it to life.

What does your decision tree look like?

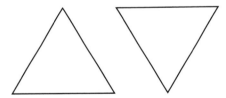

The tactical and strategic decisions of your decision tree can be established in a number of ways. Limits could take the form of a financial threshold. For instance, an automobile dealership service manager could be empowered to make decisions for unexpected repairs to any vehicle up to $2,000. The important thing is to set the conditions for decision-making, then stick with those conditions.

Empowering others may go against some of your instincts as a leader. One might even argue that now, more than ever, we have the capability to control everything. We live in an informa-tion age where smart phones, tablets, laptops, and other tech-nological innovations enable managers to maintain constant contact with their subordinates. These innovations are a dream come true for the micro-managers who can check in with team members dozens of times a day and make every decision for them. However, this practice isn't healthy for growing a culture of leaders. Instead, it creates a culture of followers.

If you're going to have a Level 5 culture, you need team members you can trust to act within your intent. This means that you won't have them lining up at the door every day to ask you for permission to do every task . And now you have time for what really matters—such as mastering the skills of "fire prevention."

There's some risk associated with this approach. In the military, as we came out of the 1970s, we realized we had to change our culture if we wanted to remain relevant. As the Cold War seemed to be drawing to a close, we were facing a tremendous number of diverse threats from different parts of the world. This meant that the military was badly needed, even while it faced internal challenges. We needed to change our culture. We had to develop junior leaders who could make far more strategic decisions. The military had to create a framework of trust and empowerment to grow young leaders who could make those kinds of decisions and then give them the authority to make decisions in a more decentralized way. This approach paid off incredibly well, as we saw during the first Gulf War and in many campaigns since that time. Our junior leaders have con-tinually stepped up above and beyond our expectations because they were trusted and empowered to make major decisions.

You must commit to the process of trusting and empowering your people. How will you know it's working? One key indi-cator is your retention rate.

Across the industry, the average turnover rate is about 39.6% a year.[25] When you translate the numbers and look at turnover in terms of cost, including recruitment, onboarding, and training, you realize that's a lot of money. A recent study showed that, in the case of entry level employees, it typically costs an employer between 30% and 50% of their annual salary to replace them. The expense goes up dramatically from there. For mid-level employees, it costs 150% of their annual salary to replace them. For high level employees, the cost is 400% of their salary.[26] Replacing people is about more than money. There's a very high cost in terms of time and energy associated with turnover, too, which should give you one more reason to retain team members and grow them whenever possible.

One of the indicators that trust and empowerment are present in your organization is that people want to be a part of your team. They feel as though they are valued. This is a hugely powerful component of a Level 5 culture. That sense of belonging translates into vastly improved retention rates, leading to money saved and an improved team morale.

---

25 Personnel turnover can vary widely from one industry another. According to Wikipedia, "In the United States, the average total of non-farm seasonally adjusted monthly turnover was 3.3% for the period from December, 2000 to November, 2008.[3] However, rates vary widely when compared over different periods of time and with different job sectors. For example, during the 2001-2006 period, the annual turnover rate for all industry sectors averaged 39.6% prior to seasonal adjustments,[4] while the Leisure and Hospitality sector experienced an average annual rate of 74.6% during this same period.[5]"

26 This data comes from an article by Karlyn Borysenko "What Was Management Thinking? The High Cost of Personnel Turnover" which appeared in *eremedia.com* April 22, 2015.

Principle 4: Do the Right Thing When No One is Looking

Our next principle, "Do the right thing when no one is looking," translates exceptionally well into the Level 5 ecosystem. When you develop that level of excellence in the organization, people *want* to do the right thing. More importantly, they're willing to keep doing it even when nobody is around to watch them. What do you do to create that environment where people are going to do the right thing?

So far, we've discussed some of the other components of doing right, including the principle of setting the azimuth, the principle of listening, and the principle of trust and empower. The manifestations of these three principles help create the conditions that will support many team members in doing the right things—and doing those right things all the time—because they feel as though they *belong*. It's critically important to recognize team members for doing right. While we often tell our team members, "Good job," it has become an empty phrase.

One of the most powerful tools to reinforce positive behaviors is the handwritten note. It's simple, but tremendously effective. All it requires is about 20 seconds of your time to jot down a quick note onto a piece of personal stationery. For instance, you could write, *"Hi Kim, I really appreciate the way you delivered the presentation in our last staff meeting. I thought it was clear, concise, and very effective. Thanks for your good work!"* Talk is cheap, but a note takes time and intention, and it can serve as a visual reminder for recipients. In an email world, a handwritten note takes only one extra moment, but that thoughtfulness goes a long way!

This practice will reinforce positive behaviors and encourage people to do the right thing. You'll often find your notes under the glass at people's desks, on the walls of cubicles, etc. We've even seen people put them in scrapbooks. Recognition also serves to empower your team members so they'll feel more confident when making decisions. When you spend much of your time recognizing doing right, more right happens. You're well on your way to having a Level 5 culture.

Principle 5: When in Charge, Take Charge

Our next principle is "When in charge, take charge." It doesn't mean you always need to be out front barking orders. Being in charge means accepting the responsibility entrusted to you and acting accordingly. In some cases, taking charge means empowering people. In others, it's developing a stronger listening environment. When in charge, you're always leading from the decisive point, and establishing the conditions for others to make good decisions.

A healthy culture is one where leaders are constantly curious. They're asking questions and listening to concerns. They're paying attention to their surroundings and are willing to change their plans when needed. As we all know, few plans ever survive the first shot or action step. You must demonstrate flexibility when in charge.

Leaders who are in charge are paying attention. They adapt as conditions change. I used to think that once I'd written a plan, I should stick to it regardless of any changing conditions. However, I soon discovered through painful experience that when you do that, you're probably going to fail. I certainly did more than once.

I remember once as a Squadron Commander at the National Training Center at Fort Irwin, California, I had devised a tactical plan for an attack on the opposing forces we were battling against in the Mojave Desert. As we got closer to the designated time for the attack, it became clear that the enemy was massing his forces at the exact location we had intended to attack. Unmoved by reality, I was determined to follow my plan, despite the entreaties by my staff to adjust it.

As the battle unfolded, I quickly saw that we were in a fierce battle of attrition, where the defending enemy had a distinct advantage. He could stay in place and defend from prepared positions, but we had to cross the open desert and attack. The fighting raged to a standstill, ending in a draw. We had been lucky to achieve that outcome, given the critical mistake I had made by attacking his strength instead of his weakness.

At the After Action Review following the battle, all of us gathered in a large tent to review the operation. After going through the plan and the execution, there was little doubt we had missed a golden opportunity for success because of my stubborn refusal to adjust the plan. As I stood up in front of the soldiers of the unit, I knew what I had to say.

"Guys," I told them, "You were exceptional out there in the fight. I let you down because I did not adapt." There was silence in the tent. They knew I was right: it was on me. But I vowed I would not make that mistake again, and we won every battle that followed.

Taking charge isn't about poking people in the chest and saying, "Do this, do that." Instead, try this: "Here's what we're facing. What do you all think is the best way to get at this?" And then, once a decision has been reached, saying, "Let's pull together to make it work." That's the kind of calm, deliberate presence and teamwork that taking charge really represents.

Leaders who take charge when in charge delegate authority, but *not* responsibility. When things go wrong, the leader owns the mistakes. When things go well, the team shares the success and credit.

Principle 6: Balance the Personal and Professional

The last of our Big 6™ principles which can help to build a Level 5 culture is one of the great cornerstones of all healthy cultures: "Balance the personal and professional." Healthy cultures are cultures where people understand the importance of living according to their values. If you map out what you do during the course of a day or week and compare it to your personal values, you'll probably discover a gap. Part of the problem is caused by those Low Value Meetings I talked about earlier, but the other part is because we, as individuals, aren't focused on paying attention to the things we value the most. We'll talk about them, but that doesn't mean we're living according to them in terms of where and how we spend our time, energy, and effort.

Across an organization, the culture should reflect your collective values. If your organization has gone through the process of setting the azimuth and hasn't then operated within that framework, you can imagine people are going to be frustrated. If you notice your teammates or colleagues showing physical signs of stress, it's probably an indication that something is out of balance. Balance isn't about time. It's not about work. It's about energy.

We essentially have four kinds of energy inside us. Those energies are physical, mental, emotional, and spiritual. All four energies need to be charged or maintained, almost like a set of internal batteries. If they aren't maintained at a sufficient charge, you'll see indications pretty quickly.

If a person's physical energy is low, their performance is going to reflect that. Causes for low physical energy include a lack of physical fitness, poor dietary habits, and erratic sleeping patterns. (By the way, people always think that they eat a lot healthier than they actually do!) When your people aren't taking care of their bodies—particularly when they're forgoing sleep—their work tends to be sloppier. Because sloppy work often needs to be redone, you don't really gain productivity by asking team members to work late or respond to emails or calls well into the evening. Signs of physical fatigue include a lack of eye contact, a lack of smiling, and inattention to detail. The presence of exhausted team members also affects the morale of others around them, who may find that in addition to their imperfect work product, exhausted team members are less patient, kind, or present.

If somebody's emotional energy is low, you'll see pretty obvious indicators as well. These indications include mood swings and an extremely short temper. They will also face a lack of creative ideas, where they may have once been amazing contributors. One red flag is email tone. If a person suddenly starts writing emails that are either insulting, derisive, or characterized by an over-use of capital letters and emoticons, it's often a sign that the person is under some emotional stress. These are issues that need to be dealt with before they get worse.

Contrary to how it might sound, a person's spiritual energy isn't necessarily a matter of their religion or psyche. Instead, it's about a sense of belief and belonging, which includes devoting some time and energy to nurturing the spirit. Some people accomplish this through meditation. Others choose walks in nature or journaling. Even something as simple as reflecting on the day's events before you go to bed can be incredibly helpful when it comes to figuring out how you can accomplish things in a more effective manner and improve the way you communicate.

While the other three levels of energy are important when it comes to sustaining a person's performance, mental energy is what will drive real progress in the journey to a Level 5 culture. Your mental battery is charged through learning and various forms of self-improvement. We've often heard it said that the best leaders are lifelong learners. They make a hobby out of reading, studying, and learning about new things. They're always seeking new ways to grow personally and profession- ally. These leaders have a passion for knowledge; they're always keen to share new ideas that they've read about. Many of them are writers themselves. One of the hallmarks of great leaders is that they write professionally to share knowledge across the field or industry in which they operate. To achieve a mental balance in your organization, you must support people's efforts to learn and grow mentally.

The four kinds of energy inside us are the best indicators of the balance that we have as individuals. Demonstrating these types of balance as leaders encourages them within our teams. In turn, these balance levels cascade across the organization and its culture through how everyone respects the four levels, nur- tures them, and supports programs to sustain balance. There are a number of efforts that you and your team members can undertake—engaging in healthier lifestyle choices, celebrat- ing family activities (births, graduations, etc.), educating the workforce on the benefits of meditating—which will promote personal balance. If your organization respects and promotes these efforts, then you're going to achieve a level of balance within the organization as a whole.

This balance will be sustained because your team members are going to look out for one another. For instance, if they notice somebody looks tired every afternoon, they might suggest taking a walk together at lunch each day. In the same way, teammates encourage one another to read more or learn about something new, sharing articles that excite them to help the team enhance its knowledge. You'll notice a collective effort across the organization to promote balance when your culture is moving toward a new level of excellence.

The Power of the First Impression

One of the most important ways you can determine if your culture is moving in the right direction is to review and adjust your onboarding process. Whenever a new person joins your team, he or she will be exposed in that first impression to your organization's culture and see how the Big 6™ principles manifest themselves in your behaviors. They will probably spend time working alongside an experienced member of the team to observe their actions and learn how things are done. Onboarding your new recruits in a careful, deliberate manner gives them a much higher chance of assimilating the key components of your culture up front.

Unfortunately, we sometimes treat onboarding as a checklist procedure, right? It's something we do using a clipboard (or the electronic equivalent). Usually the HR team monitors the clipboard, and we consider ourselves successful at this task when all the blocks get checked within a certain time frame for each new hire.

This checklist procedure usually fails to create the right first impression when someone joins the team. According to a recent article in *Process Street* by Benjamin Brandall, "The most important piece of the puzzle when it comes to retaining your best employees is the onboarding process. Why? Because first impressions *count for everything*."[27] It stands to reason, then, that doing it poorly will cause a ripple effect, setting conditions for even those with the most potential to quickly start looking elsewhere.

Here are four proven techniques to set yourself and your company up for success in keeping the good people you've worked so hard to find:

1. **Use Leaders and Peers for Onboarding**. The initial welcome is not a task you delegate. As the senior leader, make it a point to personally conduct the initial welcome. But then make it a team effort to bring in new members in a deliberate way, starting with positive, personal interaction.

2. **Make Onboarding a Performance Objective**. Describe what you expect of your leaders and team members in bringing in new people effectively.

3. **Conduct a Debrief** (After Action Review) after each onboarding. Collect the team and review what worked well, what didn't work per plan, and what to do to get better.

4. **Ask the New Team Member for Input**. Use a survey 30-60 days after a new member comes on board to see how she thinks she was brought in and prepared for her new responsibilities. Make sure to ask what she wishes was included in her initial onboarding! Include expectations, too. Then, act on the results.

---

27 Benjamin Brandall wrote a number of articles in 2016 on the onboarding process and how effective use of the process reduces turnover and increases buy-in.

This approach is far more effective than the traditional checklist procedure, or even worse, just showing them to a desk and computer and letting them figure out the rest. Leaving a new hire to their own devices means that they're far less likely to understand your culture, let alone buy into it. A bad first impression is almost impossible to undo.

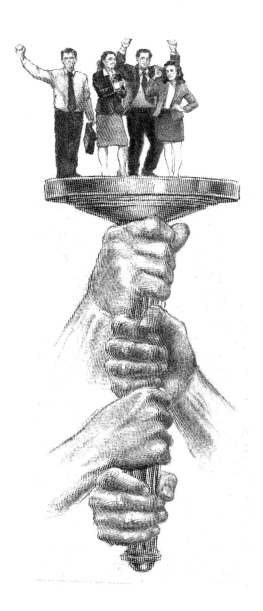

Chapter 6:
When Teams Permit Toxicity

Before we get into the specific characteristics of different levels of culture, let's spend a little more time discussing the concept of culture.

Culture is a balanced blend of human psychology, attitudes, actions, and beliefs that combined create either pleasure or pain, serious momentum or miserable stagnation. A strong culture flourishes with a clear set of values and norms that actively guide the way a company operates. Employees are actively and passionately engaged in the business, operating from a sense of confidence and empowerment rather than navigating their days through miserably extensive procedures and mind-numbing bureaucracy. Performance-oriented cultures possess statistically better financial growth, with high employee involvement, strong internal communication, and an acceptance of a healthy level of risk-taking in order to achieve new levels of innovation.

Misunderstood and Mismanaged

Culture, like brand, is misunderstood and often discounted as a touchy-feely component of business that belongs to HR. It's not intangible or fluffy, it's not a vibe or the office décor. It's one of the most important drivers that has to be set or adjusted to push long-term, sustainable success. It's not good enough just to have an amazing product and a healthy bank balance. Long-term success is dependent on a culture that is nurtured and alive. Culture is the environment in which your strategy and your brand thrives or dies a slow death.

Think about it like a nurturing habitat for success. Culture cannot be manufactured. It has to be genuinely nurtured by everyone from the CEO down. Ignoring the health of your culture is like letting aquarium water get dirty.[28]

"So, what are the signs that the water is getting dirty?" According to Jim Riley, writing for the British company tutor2u, various experts have looked at this question and highlighted common symptoms of a toxic culture. In his words these include:

- **Weak leadership:** A team with no clear sense of direction is an indication of weak leadership.

- **Double standards**: If there are members of leadership who don't hold themselves accountable to the same standards and expectations as others in the business, the culture will soon be based on contempt.

---

28 "Culture Eats Strategy for Lunch" by Shawn Parr in *Fast Company*, January 24, 2012, p. 1–29.

- **Authoritarian or bullying leadership**: If the leadership are bullies, then those who succeed in such a culture are likely to be bullies, too. Authoritarian leadership too often creates a culture of fear and subservience.

- **Absence of openness and honesty**: Can everyone speak his/her mind? The alternative is a culture where important issues are swept under the carpet.

- **Lack of transparency and morality**

- **Dishonesty and corruption**: The root of this culture is often ambition or greed.

- **Reluctance to embrace change**: This can create a stifling environment where innovation and creativity are discouraged.

- **Rampant gossip/rumors**: The rumors could be about other employees, leadership, or strategy. But they spread quickly and can have devastating effects.

- **Us/them mentality**

- **Retaining poor-performing staff**: Keeping them on board will frustrate the good performers with good attitudes, who will be much more likely to leave.

When these toxic habits and activities are translated into a workplace, the results can be shocking. Over the long-term, these teams can permit or even encourage harm to their staff, their environment, or their consumers. The following examples are not for the faint of heart:

Goldman Sachs

When financial analyst Greg Smith left Goldman Sachs in 2012, he wrote in the OpEd section of *The New York Times*: "I believe

I have worked here long enough to understand the trajectory of its culture, its people and its identity. And I can honestly say that the environment now is as toxic and destructive as I have ever seen it. ... The firm has veered so far from the place I joined right out of college that I can no longer in good conscience say that I identify with what it stands for."[29]

Here was one of the iconic companies on Wall Street that had fallen from grace, allowing its culture to decay to the point where many of the most talented analysts in the world, like Greg Smith, could no longer tolerate working there—and over 3 million readers read his comments.

Australian Olympic Swimming Team at London 2012

Australia has traditionally enjoyed great success through world-class performance in Olympic swimming meets. So what went wrong at London 2012?

The Australian team managed to win just one gold medal, despite being tapped for huge success. An independent review (commissioned by Swimming Australia in the wake of the team's poor performance in London) found a failure of leadership and culture with Australian swimming's worst Olympics in two decades undermined by a lack of moral authority and discipline which manifested in a "schoolyard clamor for attention and influence."

Australia's 2012 Olympic swimming team was consumed by a "toxic" culture involving bullying, the misuse of prescription drugs, and a lack of discipline, the damning report found. The

---

29   "Why I'm Leaving Goldman Sachs" by Greg Smith in the OpEd section of the *New York Times*, March 14, 2012.

independent review cited incidents of "getting drunk, misuse of prescription drugs, breaching curfews, deceit, bullying."[30]

Barclays

Barclays was one of several leading banks that were implicated in a scandal involving the fixing of the Libor interest rate. Whistle-blowers pointed to a culture of fear that allowed the practice to go on. The Serious Fraud Office launched a criminal inquiry into interest rate fixing amid increasing clamor for rogue bankers to be prosecuted. The Libor scandal was a key factor in the appointment of Antony Jenkins as the new CEO of Barclays. One of his first actions was to commission an independent review into the culture at Barclays which he clearly feared was turning toxic.

The subsequent Salz Review blamed "cultural shortcomings" at the bank for problems that led to the Libor-rigging scandal. The Salz Review said the bank needed a "transformational change" to restore its reputation among the public. The review said the bank had become too focused on profit and bonuses rather than the interests of customers."[31]

Baylor Football

Recently, Baylor University released the scathing findings of fact from the school-commissioned investigation by law firm Pepper Hamilton into a sexual violence scandal on its campus.[32] The scandal included months of media reporting on alleged acts of violence against women by roughly a dozen football players,

---

30 "Organisational Culture: Toxic Culture and Business Performance," by Jim Riley in *tutor2u*, February 27, 2015, pp. 1–4.

31 Ibid

32 *SB Nation*, May 26, 2016.

with accusations that the school and athletic department had responded ineffectively.

That came alongside the school's announcement that head coach, Art Briles, was being fired, while school president, Ken Starr, and athletic director, Ian McCaw, faced punishment, among others. The university also self-reported these violations to the NCAA, and has announced it would cooperate with college athletics' operating body.

According to the report, Baylor football staff, including unnamed coaches, prevented meaningful investigation of multiple accusations of sexual assault and dating violence by failing to report them outside of the athletic department. Football staffers also did things that "gave the illusion of responsiveness to complainants but failed to provide a meaningful institutional response under Title IX." Those included:

- Meeting personally with victims or their parents and subsequently failing to report the misconduct

- Conducting internal investigations without training or authority, "which improperly discredited complainants and denied them the right to a fair, impartial and informed investigation"

- Actively diverting cases from criminal investigation or Baylor's student conduct review

These issues were not unknown to the university's administrators. Other departments "repeatedly raised concerns that the Athletics Department's response to student or employee misconduct was inadequate."

The effect of the football staff's abhorrent actions, and the administration's failure to change them, was an overall belief that Baylor football operated under its own set of rules. Baylor has been criticized for its acceptance of transfer Sam Ukwuachu, from Boise State, who was later convicted of raping a fellow Baylor athlete. Baylor also accepted Shawn Oakman from Penn State, who would be reportedly investigated during his playing career at Baylor and arrested afterward for a separate incident, both for alleged crimes against women.

Questions about what Baylor knew about Ukwuachu's dismissal from Boise State remain, and the report's abstract does not name Briles or any coaches individually. But it is highly critical of Baylor's efforts in screening transfers. The report says Baylor did not consistently conduct due diligence via "background checks, requesting records of prior college disciplinary actions and character reference screening forms." Importantly, it says Baylor did not consistently follow its own "previously implemented processes." But this went beyond football.

Pepper found that Baylor's efforts to implement Title IX were slow, ad hoc, and hindered by a lack of institutional support and engagement by senior leadership. Based on a high-level audit of all reports of sexual harassment or violence for three academic years from 2012-2013 through 2014-2015, Pepper found that the University's student conduct processes were wholly inadequate to consistently provide a prompt and equitable response under Title IX. Baylor failed to consistently support complainants through the provision of interim measures, and that in some cases, the University failed to take action to identify and eliminate a potential hostile environment, prevent its recurrence, or address its effects for individual complainants or the broader campus community.

Pepper also found examples of actions by University administrators that directly discouraged complainants from reporting or participating in student conduct processes, or that contributed to or accommodated a hostile environment. In one instance, those actions constituted retaliation against a complainant for reporting sexual assault."[33]

---

33 Ibid.

Chapter 7:
Climbing the Levels

Over the course of four decades, I've been exposed to each of the five levels of culture described in the succeeding pages. For brevity's sake, I've given each one a descriptor which highlights its key characteristic:

Level 1: The "Nametag" culture

This ecosystem is a loose confederation of self-centered individuals, who act in their own personal interests.

Level 2: The "Follower" culture

This environment is one where there are few leaders and many followers, and only those with tangible ownership are vested in the welfare of the company.

Level 3: The "Points of Light" culture

This culture is characterized by a few individuals who are personally aligned with the values of the organization; however, most are just doing a job and performing the associated tasks with that job.

Level 4: The "Coalition of the Willing" culture

The coalition culture has a large population of those who want the organization to be successful, and align their personal goals and aspirations with those of the company.

Level 5: The "We're All In" culture

This is the culture of excellence, characterized by fully committed team members who see their personal success and fulfillment in the achievement of the organization's goals and objectives.

Let's take a moment to look at these types closely. See if you can identify your organization as we unpack each level.

The Level 1 Culture: Nametag

The toxicity highlighted earlier emerged from cultures with the wrong values. The leaders of these organizations were clearly not vested in the health of the culture; thus these examples represent what I call "Nametag" cultures. As John C. Maxwell describes in the way some Level 1 leaders operate, people perform at a level where they feel they can do the least. Maxwell highlights the values challenge for Level 1 leaders by telling this Mark Twain story:

"In a speech on the value of honesty, Mark Twain once told this story: 'When I was a boy, I was walking along a street and happened to spy a cart full of watermelons. I was fond of watermelon, so I sneaked quietly on the cart and snitched one. Then I ran into a nearby alley and sank my teeth into the melon. No sooner had I done so, however, then a strange feeling came over me. Without a moment's hesitation, I made my decision.

I walked back to the cart, replaced the melon—and took a ripe one."[34]

Most of us have at least had a glimpse at a Nametag culture somewhere along the way. Some companies and organizations with these cultures are reasonably successful for a while, at least from a Profit and Loss (P&L) standpoint, but there are toxic undercurrents which rapidly unhinge that success at some point.

Nametag cultures don't have a clear azimuth. There may or may not be a mission statement. If there is one, it was probably written by one person and no one else knows what it is. The leader's intent, values, and behaviors are not commonly understood, and that's understandable since most likely they have never been discussed.

There's no strategic planning process to help align the organization, either. Nametag cultures do what they've always done and that becomes their strategy. Like the Cheshire Cat tells Alice in Lewis Carroll's *Alice in Wonderland*, "If you don't know where you're going, any road will get you there."

Listening is rare in Nametag cultures. Most of the leaders just transmit messages, usually parroting what their boss told them. Mistakes are common because people do what they thought they heard. Most meetings are Low Value Meetings, without any format, agenda, or deliverables. And in those meetings only one person (the leader) speaks. Everyone else is either afraid to speak up or believes no one wants to hear his or her opinion.

Trust and empowerment are absent in Nametag cultures. High turnover is the norm. Rumors abound. There's no succession

---

34 John C. Maxwell, *The 5 Levels of Leadership: Proven Steps to Maximize Your Potential*, New York: Center Street Press, 2011, pp. 45–46.

planning, as it's easy to "just hire someone else" when management doesn't truly value its team. The coffee pot is a focal point for toxic conversations. Money is considered to be the most important incentive. In fact, for many, it's the only incentive.

Doing the right thing is a foreign term in Nametag cultures. Most of the time team members do what they can get away with. Beating the system becomes the way of life, and for most it's a matter of pride to do it better than others. Most won't share information because knowledge is seen as job security. Silos are firmly entrenched in the Nametag culture.

The only person in charge in Nametag cultures is the one who signs the checks. As in the examples cited earlier, the water in the aquarium becomes dirty. In the absence of instructions, the workforce typically does nothing for fear of being wrong if they act. Everyone learns to tolerate toxicity. And since turnover is high, people in the Nametag culture understand there's no such thing as job security.

Balance simply means a mass exodus from the parking lot no later than 5:01 PM. Leaders in a Nametag culture know little or nothing about the families, hobbies, or outside interests of their team members—nor do they care. As long as the job gets done, there's no corporate interest in the well-being of the individuals in the workforce. They can't relate "people investment" to the bottom line.

The Nametag culture is all about "me and mine." It is by its very nature self-centered and focused on the welfare of a few at the expense of others. It's not a question of *if* the culture will implode—it's just a question of *when*.

The Level 2 Culture: Follower

"Followers can be defined by their behavior—doing what others want them to do....They generally go along to get along, particularly with those in higher positions. In the workplace, they may comply so as not to put money or stature at risk. In the community, they may comply to preserve collective stability and security—or simply because it's the easiest thing to do."[35]

When we talk about a culture of "Followers," we are describing an ecosystem built around that mindset. Follower cultures are healthier than Nametag cultures, but it's still not the kind of aquarium most of us want to swim in. The leadership in these organizations is highly centralized, very controlling, and therefore not the least bit empowering. For the leadership, it's all about the status quo.

If we look at the Follower culture in terms of the Big 6™, we see only a few incremental improvements from the stark world of Nametag. Leaders in the Follower culture don't set a true azimuth. They might write a mission statement, and maybe a vision statement to go along with it, but they only really exist on the wall above the receptionist's desk or in the conference room.

Listening is not a priority in the Follower culture. Leaders rarely circle back to see if what they thought they said was heard that way. Frequently, mistakes occur because the intent is often not clearly communicated, much less understood across the team, department, or company.

Trust and empowerment aren't common, either. The Follower culture is based on rules and procedures. The more the merrier. The operative word in the Follower culture is *compliance*. There's

---

35 Barbara Kellerman, "What Every Leader Needs to Know About Followers," in the *Harvard Business Review* (December 2007), p. 1.

not much room for trust because the "how" is prescribed. People in the Follower workforce are expected to follow the rules, and when rules are missing they wait for someone to write them before they act. There's a high degree of comfort in the Follower culture. All you have to do is follow the standard operating procedures and you can't be wrong.

Doing the right thing is OK—as long as it's part of the rules. If nobody's looking, then you're on your own. If someone is looking, Followers are expected to comply with the rules—and report those who don't. There's little or no mutual accountability among Followers. The leaders hold people accountable by using the rules and regulations to effectively beat them into submission, and in organizations with a large number of specified procedures, it's usually not difficult to find mistakes. High turnover and low morale are common, and the cultural learning curve is almost always steep as new people are constantly showing up to replace those who were non-compliant.

The ones in charge are tenured, not talented. They occupy their positions because they've been in the company forever. Government bureaucracies are classic Follower cultures. Longevity is king. For many, the "Peter Principle" has already kicked in.[36] They've exceeded their level of competency and, because they either know the boss or pose no immediate threat, they're firmly entrenched in their positions. Followers have no intention of developing other leaders. Instead, they're quite content growing followers. As in the Nametag culture, the environment is characterized by a lack of opportunity, not the development of opportunity.

---

36 The "Peter Principle" is a concept in management theory formulated by Laurence J. Peter in 1969, and it says that leaders are promoted based on their performance in their current roles, and not in accordance with their potential to fill the higher position. So, incompetence ultimately kicks in.

Few long-term initiatives stick because this is a flavor-of-the-month culture. The boss might have a good idea because he or she went on vacation or to a meeting in another town. However, these ideas quickly fizzle out. This short-term perspective frustrates team members because they'll have started out on a new project or initiative for a few weeks only to see momentum falter before it can even really get underway.

Here's a story relayed to me which demonstrates the destructive potential of the Good Idea Fairy (GIF) at work in a Follower culture:

> I remember sitting in a meeting with my boss (VP), his boss (SVP/CFO) and the GIF at XXX Bank many years ago. The GIF vocalized an idea through the CFO. Back in our offices, the VP dropped everything else and pushed the team to plan and strategize around the idea. We probably spent three man weeks coming up with a plan, a schedule, a budget, an executive presentation, the works. When we took it back to the CFO he said, 'What's this?' He didn't even remember the idea, and certainly didn't expect us to act on it. Lesson learned…[37]

As a result, morale in Follower organizations tends to be very low. No one respects the concept of balance. Work is work, and thereby completely separate from off duty time. Few leaders know the names of the family members of their employees. Fun is not part of the workday. Eye contact is rare, as are smiles.

Followers endure Low Value Meetings where they're assigned an endless series of projects that they know will likely never be

---

[37] An actual story recounted to me by a bank executive in response to my February 2017 blog, "Where the GIF Lives."

finished. Teams will be put together for those projects, but those teams will be under-resourced and the team leaders won't be given a charter with authority, both of which limit how much the team can actually do. In many cases, the team leaders really aren't even leading; instead, they're doing little more than gathering data and reporting it to a boss.

Companies with a Follower culture typically promote on the basis of favoritism or longevity. As with a Nametag culture, if there is some system in place to evaluate performance, it's not being used. It most likely sits on the shelf and maybe makes an appearance once per year during an annual performance review; but, even then it's more a matter of checking boxes on a standardized form. The "Peter Principle' is alive and well here.

In a Follower culture, everybody is just trying to survive. When there are flashes of opportunity, the sparks always flicker out. Followers comply with an ever-increasing body of rules and procedures, and those that don't follow the rules go away. Longevity is the key to opportunity, and a flavor-of-the-month attitude keeps the workforce jumping from one fleeting "good idea" to the next, based on the whims of the leadership and the Good Idea Fairy. It's a compliance-driven ecosystem, and in the competitive, uncertain world we live in, at some point it's almost certain to fail.

The Level 3 Culture: Points of Light

The Level 3 "Points of Light" culture is the first one where visionary leadership and application of the Big 6™ principles emerge. It's a culture with potential, but it also has considerable friction against change. As it exists today, the organization is still likely to face high turnover and ethical pitfalls.

In the Points of Light culture there is usually some type of azimuth established, but it's not always commonly understood across the organization. These organizations may have a mission statement, but it is likely to be ineffective, because it is not specific about who they are, what they do, and why they do it. Odds are that it's more along the lines of: "We do stuff." A Points of Light culture's values generally aren't clearly defined and expected behaviors aren't captured in writing. It's assumed that everyone knows them. And that leads to some unfortunate outcomes.

In the Points of Light culture, listening is selective. There is still a strong tendency for the leader to speak first rather than last, and Low Value Meetings remain the most common type. One-on-one meetings are few and far between. Typically the leaders don't ask meaningful questions in or out of meetings, so they don't get useful information. Sound decision-making is more hit and miss than routine.

Trust and empowerment is reserved for selected individuals and teams. Employees popular with the boss or the C-Suite team will get to lead a couple of projects here and there, often just as a means of placating them or getting things off the boss's plate. Some will be given a little more opportunity, something to excite them, and a little more resources to go along with it in an attempt to get them to stick around. Of course, these token gestures don't work for long and, before you know it, the high potential individuals are shopping their resumes.

Points of Light leaders are fully capable of making deliberate decisions that are deeply flawed, completely against what we expect in a healthy organizational culture. A classic example is the case of the Ford Pinto. In the 1970s, the Ford Pinto made headlines for being one of the vehicles involved in a series of horrific crashes because the car's engineering was flawed. The gas tank would often explode when hit from the rear. In the aftermath of the scandal, the decision process that led to the Pinto's faulty design was scrutinized.

Under intense competition from Volkswagen, Ford had rushed the Pinto into production in a significantly shorter time period than was usually the case. The potential danger of ruptured fuel tanks was discovered in preproduction crash tests, but with the assembly line ready to go, the decision was made to manufacture the car anyway. That decision was based on a cost-benefit analysis which weighed the minimal cost of repairing the fault (about $11 per vehicle at the time) against the cost of paying damages in lawsuits following accidents. Ford deemed it would be cheaper to pay damages than to make the fixes. The Pinto was manufactured with its faulty design for eight more years.

Two prominent authors who examined the Pinto case in some detail summarized it this way:

"We suspect that none of the Ford executives who were involved in this now-notorious decision would have predicted in advance that they would make such an unethical choice. Nonetheless, they made a choice that maimed and killed many people. Why? It appears that, at the time of the decision, they viewed it as a "business decision" rather than an "ethical decision."[38]

This story serves as a sad testimony to how easily a Points of Light culture can drift into doing the wrong thing by being able to change (or compromise) their values and then rationalize their decisions. These authors called the process "ethical fading."

---

38   Bazerman and Tenbrunsel, *Blind Spots*, 2011, p.14-15.

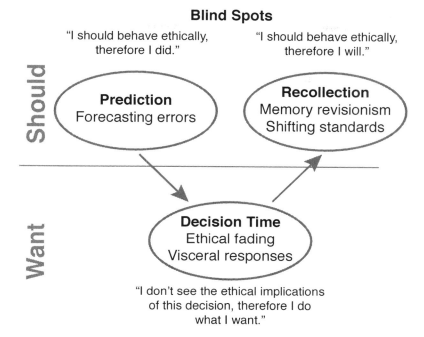

Blind Spots

In the Points of Light culture, only a few have the opportunity to take charge. The decision tree is typically upside down. Because information is so readily accessible, higher level decision makers are reluctant to give up control. Many young, promising leaders who could truly be the "points of light" for the future are denied the opportunity.

Points of Light leaders hire talent in lieu of developing it. Turnover is high because new people are continually coming into the organization, and they don't assimilate smoothly into the culture. When promotions do happen, they are usually based on performance, not potential. For example, a high performing salesperson often becomes the sales manager, even when he might lack the capability or desire to lead. Failure usually results, and both the individual and the organization suffer. The cycle thus perpetuates itself.

Leader development, mentoring, and coaching are typically episodic. Some program leaders embrace the concept of growing leaders, but they're outnumbered. They are, indeed, points of light who could lead change. The challenge is they are usually surrounded by darkness. If unsupported by the senior leadership, their energy wanes and they revert to the mean.

Points of Light cultures are similarly ignorant of the importance of balance. Since the leaders lack understanding of the 4 kinds of energy resident in both individuals and teams, they focus instead on time. Most leaders will at least encourage people to come to work on time and leave on time, and they consider that good enough to promote and sustain balance. At the same time, these leaders will look for workers who stay late and come in on weekends as the hard chargers, so the culture suffers from a perceived double standard of "says" versus "does."

Some Points of Light cultures develop wellness initiatives and other "battery-charging" promotional initiatives which are usually more talk than action. When one or two people make positive life choices—like exercising or going on a healthier diet—the celebration is short lived.

With few exceptions, Points of Light leaders are only casually engaged in growing the culture. Unless the leadership is persistent and the "points of light" high potential young leaders are engaged and supported by the senior stakeholders, the selected opportunities come...and go, unrealized.

The Level 4 Culture: Coalition of the Willing

On the other hand, Coalition of the Willing cultures are much healthier. The majority of team members have bought into the company's goals and objectives as their own. The right values are beginning to come to life in the ecosystem.

Now the azimuth is much more well defined and clearly understood across the team. The mission in a Level 4 culture establishes the who, what, and why of the organization. There are initial outlines of the intent, too. The leadership in the Coalition of the Willing culture asks questions like, "Where are we going in the next six months or the next year?" and "Do we have milestones established to get there?" Management plans are then established to accomplish those milestones.

There's an outcomes-based strategic planning process in place. Even though the formal process may not take place annually, it's reviewed on a periodic basis. This creates a much higher sense of alignment than is the case in Levels 1 through 3 cultures. This alignment creates the potential to become a Level 5 culture of excellence.

In terms of the rest of the Big 6™ principles, a Coalition of the Willing organization has many of the healthy qualities of looking beyond today, tomorrow, and next week. They're looking out towards a longer-term end state. People see themselves as having the opportunity for a career rather than just a job. The leadership is invested in the long-term health of the organization.

This investment by the leadership stands in stark contrast to Levels 1 through 3 where there's much more of a tendency to ignore internal potential and hire outside talent. Consequently, internal promotion rates in a Coalition of the Willing culture are much higher. As young leaders grow and receive greater responsibilities, senior leaders provide mentorship and coaching.

Active listening is much more common in a Coalition of the Willing culture. There's much more effort put into feedback mechanisms and one-on-one sessions. Leaders teach and practice asking effective questions. This emphasis on effective listening helps to give the leadership a better idea of where the organization is, where it's going, and the progress being made to get there.

Trust and empowerment really begin to take shape in Coalition of the Willing cultures. There are decision mechanisms in place, and junior leaders are much more empowered to make decisions because the senior leadership is willing to underwrite some mistakes. That typically doesn't occur in the Level 1, 2, and 3 cultures where, if they underwrite a mistake at all, they'll only underwrite it at a very low level where there is little risk. Those lower level cultures don't afford junior leaders the opportunity to learn from what we call "sins of commission" where you're trying to do right and you simply didn't do it well. By contrast, leaders in the Coalition of the Willing cultures view mistakes as teachable moments, and leaders use the opportunities to positively build their team.

Typically, in a Level 4 culture, leaders at every level employ the backbrief technique of confirming that messages sent were understood, and they insist on conducting after-action reviews (AARs) after every major project or event. In the AARs, leaders ask:

- What did we just do successfully or unsuccessfully?

- What happened and why did it happen?

- What are we going to do about it?

- Who's responsible for doing it and when?

Everyone participates in the review; leaders check their egos at the door.

Coalition of the Willing cultures have a lot of people who do the right thing when no one is looking. They take action to ensure that safety, security, and discipline exist across the company or organization. The leaders are willing to pitch in and do the same work that the team members are doing, if necessary. They're willing to get their hands dirty.

When I was a young lieutenant in what was then called West Germany, I was placed in charge of a platoon of 41 soldiers. During the day, when we weren't patrolling the East-West German border, we worked on maintaining our equipment. We had ten vehicles in the platoon. These vehicles were mechanized tanks, personnel carriers, and mortars, all of which required a lot of maintenance. Many of them had suffered battle damage in Vietnam before being shipped to Germany, which meant that we were patching up equipment which had previously been patched up. When we finished the maintenance day, or motor pool operations, we'd form up as a platoon and march back down to the barracks for the evening.

Sergeant Mac, my platoon's senior non-commissioned officer, had served multiple tours in Vietnam. He was a big, intimidating-looking man. One day soon after I arrived, at the end of a maintenance day, Sergeant Mac gave another sergeant the task of marching the soldiers down to the barracks. He then turned to me and said, "Sir, let me see your fingernails." I thought to myself, "We do that kind of hygiene work here? I'm in a strange Army!" But he wasn't doing a hygiene check. He wanted to see if my hands and fingernails were dirty. That day they weren't dirty enough, so he said, "Okay, sir, we have more work to do."

So we got back up on my tank and started to work on the generator. I installed a new generator while Sergeant Mac supervised, because he insisted that I had to know, and be able to do, all the tasks my soldiers did if I was going to lead them effectively.

Even with all the challenges we had in the post-Vietnam army in the mid-1970s, there were leaders like Platoon Sergeant Mac who understood what it took to develop the right culture and grow leaders who would bring the right values to life. I'm forever indebted to Sergeant Mac for the lesson that day. It instilled deep within me that leadership wasn't just about giving out instructions. This was about leading by doing, living the Army model of "Be-Know-Do."

Leaders in Coalition of the Willing cultures insist on preparing people for the next level of responsibility. Leaders seek out responsibility. They want to be at the head of projects and opportunities because they know that the senior leadership has high regard for those who step up and lead from the decisive point, whether it's the front or somewhere else.

Leaders take the time to recognize those who are doing good things. They recognize them publicly. They have ceremonies where they give people the opportunity to stand up in front of their peers and be recognized for doing the right thing. And this fosters on-going performance.

There's a true sense of balance in Coalition of the Willing cultures. The four kinds of energy—physical, emotional, mental, and spiritual—are all supported by the leadership. Leaders model the desired behaviors, such as practicing wellness, professional reading (or writing), having an active family life, celebrating milestone events in the lives of others. They don't expect their teams to define their levels of dedication by the number of hours they spend in the office.

Managers and leaders are encouraged to know the names of their team members' significant others and family members, as well as their hobbies and activities. Senior leaders often congratulate managers and team members when one of their children or spouses receives an award or other recognition. They get to know what their team members do when they aren't at work and what they enjoy. The goal is to get to know the team members as *people*, rather than just names on a roster or an organizational chart.

The Level 4 culture is healthy from the top down. They share a common goal—the success of the organization. However, it's not universal across the team, as there are still members of the workforce who are essentially going through the motions. But these mediocre performers are still operating at a higher level because of the people around them. The Coalition of the Willing culture is on the verge of being great—if they can bring the "fence sitters" to *really* join the team...

Chapter 8:
The Level 5 Culture: "All In"

Level 5 cultures are fully committed. They are alive with the Big 6™ principles. But they have another special quality that separates them from the others. Andrew Grover, the former CEO of Intel, is credited with having coined the phrase, "Only the paranoid survive." The Level 5 culture has a healthy sense of paranoia. It inspires the leadership to anticipate and embrace change.

In 1914, Sir Ernest Shackleton, British explorer, embarked on an expedition to traverse Antarctica. His recruiting ad in *The London Times* read: *"Men wanted: For hazardous journey. Small wages, bitter cold, long months of complete darkness, constant danger, safe return doubtful. Honour and recognition in case of success."* Hundreds applied for 28 crew positions.[39]

Sir Ernest Shackleton's perilous mission to the South Pole in 1914 was a classic story of leadership through uncertainty, against

---

39   As quoted in *Multipliers: How the Best Leaders Make Everyone Smarter*, by Liz Wiseman with Greg McKeown, New York: Harper Collins, 2010, p. 22.

almost overpowering odds. He developed a Level 5 culture, and built a team that would endure and overcome some of the worst conditions imaginable.

Shackleton set forth on a journey to the South Pole in December 1914, reaching the Weddell Sea in mid-January. There was unusually early ice, and on January 19th, his ship *Endurance* became frozen in the middle of an ice floe. He realized they would be trapped until the warmer weather came (which is autumn in the southern hemisphere), so on February 24 he converted the ship to a winter station. They drifted along as part of the ice floe for months. When spring arrived in September, the thawing, refreezing and movement of the ice damaged the ship's hull. Shackleton realized they would not be able to sail the ship out as he had hoped. On October 24, water began pouring into the ship.

The crew of the Imperial Trans-Arctic Expedition. Reproduced with permission by the Royal Geographical Sociaety, London, England.

Several days later they abandoned ship and set up equipment and provisions in camps on the ice and watched as on November 21, 1915, the *Endeavor* sank. They camped on the ice floe for almost 2 months, hoping it would drift towards a known source of stored supplies on Paulet Island 250 miles away. They failed numerous times to cross the vast floe and Shackleton finally decided to set up a more permanent camp on another floe hoping it would take them to Paulet. They were within 60 miles of Paulet on March 17th, 1916. They were unable to reach it and on April 9th their ice floe broke in half. Shackleton ordered the crew into 3 lifeboats to head for the nearest land. They spent 5 difficult days at sea and, exhausted, finally landed on Elephant Island, which was 346 miles away from where their ship had sunk. They had not been on land for 497 days!

Unfortunately, Elephant Island was far from shipping routes so the chance of being rescued was non-existent. Shackleton took 5 crew members with him in one of the lifeboats they had fortified to withstand an ocean trip to South Georgia, 720 nautical miles away. He took provision for 4 weeks reasoning that if they didn't reach South Georgia by then, they would be dead.

They left on April 24, getting within sight of South Georgia on May 8. Hurricane force winds kept them from landing until the next day. They were on the unoccupied side of the island. Shackleton took two of the men with him to cross the 32 miles over treacherous mountainous terrain for 36 hours to reach the whaling station on May 20th. He sent a boat to get the three men on the other side of the island and started to organize the rescue of the rest of his crew on Elephant Island. His first three attempts failed due to impassable sea ice. He finally got help from the Chilean navy and a British whaler to rescue the 22 men. They reached them on August 30, 1916. All of Shackleton's men survived the harrowing expedition due to his extraordinary leadership under very trying conditions.[40]

His expedition and the leadership lessons it demonstrates about the power of a Level 5 culture to accomplish the extraordinary are summarized by Nancy Koehn in her 2011 essay in *The New York Times*:

> Shackleton's sense of responsibility and commitment came with a great suppleness of means. To get his men home safely, he led them across ice, sea, and land with all the tools he could muster. This combination—credible commitment to a larger purpose and flexible, imaginative methods to achieve a goal—is increasingly important in our tumultuous times.[41]

There's unmistakable clarity in the Level 5 culture. The azimuth guides the actions of every person in the organization. Leaders model the behaviors, repeat the values often and create the conditions for leaders and team to have a strong "bias for action." In the absence of specific guidance, people act within the intent.

Leaders grow leaders. They celebrate the successes of those they serve. This concept of *servant* leadership is at the heart of the "All In" culture. Here's what noted author Ken Blanchard says about the importance of servant leadership to the development of that world-class culture:

> When I mention servant leadership to many organizational leaders, they think I'm talking about the inmates running the prison, pleasing everybody, or

---

40   Shackleton's heroic expedition is summarized well in Wikipedia and a number of other publications.

41   "Leadership Lessons From the Shackleton Expedition," by Nancy F. Koehn, *The New York Times* (December 24, 2011), p. 6.

some religious movement...what they don't understand is that there are two aspects of effective leadership. The first is the strategic aspect of servant leadership. Leadership is about going somewhere. If your people don't know where you want them to go, there is little chance you will get there...the second, [the] servant aspect of servant leadership [is the] operational/implementation aspect. While our research indicates that 80 to 85 percent of the impact on organizational vitality or success comes from operational leadership, without a clear organizational constitution there would be nothing to implement or serve.[42]

Servant leadership means setting the azimuth (which Blanchard refers to as the "constitution" above) and supporting the workforce in their efforts to achieve the goals set forth in that azimuth.

The "All In" culture is all ears. Everyone is paying attention. Instructions are shared in a thoughtful, deliberate way. For example, leaders in the "All In" culture understand that emails and texts are *not* the primary form of communication. They know them as a means of *sharing certain information, but not communication.* Real communication happens face to face, or at the very least virtually or by phone.

Trust is the watchword of the "All In" culture. The decision tree is right side up. Here's an example of empowerment based on that intrinsic level of trust where the decision tree is set up in an empowering way:

---

42   Ken Blanchard in his Foreword to S. Chris Edmonds' excellent book, *The Culture Engine: A Framework for Driving Results, Inspiring Your Employees, and Transforming Your World. Hoboken,* John Wiley and Sons, 2014, pp. ii-iv.

Horst Schultze, one of the founders of the Ritz-Carlton Hotels, retired a few years ago as President and CEO. During his reign, after orientation and extensive training, every employee was given a $2,000.00 discretionary fund they could use to solve a customer problem without telling anyone. They didn't even have to tell their boss. Horst loved to collect stories about using this empowerment to make a difference…one is about a businessman who was staying at one of the Ritz-Carlton properties in Atlanta.

That day he had to fly from Atlanta to Los Angeles, and then from Los Angeles to Hawaii…because the next day he was making a major speech to his international company. He was a little disorganized as he was leaving. On his way to the airport, he discovered he'd left behind his laptop computer, which contained all of the PowerPoints he needed for his presentation. He tried to change his flights, but he couldn't. So he called the Ritz-Carlton and said, "This is the room I was in, and this is where my computer was. Have housekeeping get it and overnight it to me. They have to guarantee delivery by 10 tomorrow morning, because I need it for my one o'clock speech."

The next day Shultze was wandering around the hotel, as he often did. When he got to Housekeeping, he said, "Where's Mary?" Her co-workers said, "She's in Hawaii." He said, "What's she doing there?'

He was told, "A guest left his computer in his room, and he needs it for a speech today at one o'clock—

and Mary doesn't trust overnight carrier services."[43] (She received a commendation upon her return the next day.)

There's a deep undercurrent of mutual accountability in Level 5 cultures. From the outset, team members are expected to accept and follow the rules of organizational behavior the company has established. The "All In" onboarding process is very detailed and the performance, feedback, and assessment process are continuous. From the outset, the "All In" culture is one of continuous feedback including one-on-one, face-to-face, quality conversations about each other's strengths and weaknesses as well as measuring the steps to get better. Performance objectives include standards of conduct.

When in charge, "All In" leaders take charge. They have a strong bias for action, because they know the intent and that their leaders will underwrite honest mistakes. Internal and external customers are always the priority, so decisions are focused on satisfying their needs first.

Balance is a way of life, but leaders understand the "traditional" way of treating work-life balance as an issue of time is no longer valid. In a recent article in USA Today, that reality was highlighted:

> Nearly half of all U.S. workers check email after they leave work, and 45% say they do work during non-business hours, according to a 2016 Career-Builder survey. ... One way to survive, and even thrive, is to proactively manage the expectations of others.

---

43   This story is told by Ken Blanchard in his book *Leading at a Higher Level*, Upper Saddle River, Blanchard Management Corporation, 2010, p. 50.

That means communicating clearly about our availability and coming up with strategies such as asking one of our colleagues to cover our duties while we are on vacation. Such planning ahead can help reduce stress. "Part of anxiety is feeling out of control," says psychologist Mary Alvord.[44]

The key here is to manage the levels of energy in the workforce—physical, emotional, spiritual, and mental—and leaders in the "All In" culture are specifically trained and oriented to observe the energy levels in their teams, and act quickly when the battery levels seem to be low in any of them.

Strategic planning in an "All In" culture is part and parcel of the way they do things. Annual strategic reviews are intense 2-3 day events which are carefully planned and executed. The leadership establishes Key Result Areas (KRAs) or priorities for the next three to five years, including the current year. Management plans for the current year are built from those longer term KRA initiatives. Efforts and resources are prioritized accordingly.

"All In" leaders conduct quarterly reviews of their strategic plan and KRAs. This allows them to identify where they are now. They review their milestones, outcomes, and metrics to see how much they've done to accomplish them. They also have the opportunity to figure out what they can do to facilitate a better performance or a higher return on the investment. Finally, they identify and admit any mistakes that may have been made. Change is OK.

Mistakes and successes are both considered learning opportunities. Leaders and teams gather to conduct an AAR imme-

---

44 "Overworked? Join the Club" by Laura Petrecca in *USA Today*, January 15, 2017, p. 8B.

diately after an event to determine what happened and why it happened. The team decides what to fix and who's going to take responsibility for completing the associated tasks—and when. Ultimately, they learn from each experience and bring continuous improvement to life.

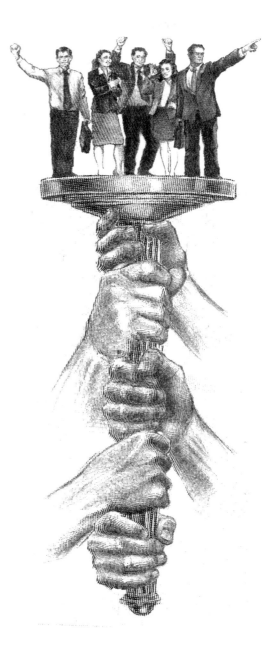

The Level 5 "All In" culture is healthy, vibrant, and attractive. Others want to be part of these organizations, and those who are in want to stay in. Excellence is the standard, improvement is expected, and pride is evident everywhere you look. People make eye contact. They smile. They conduct High Value Meetings. Leaders embrace the certainty of uncertainty because they understand it is the reality of the world we live in.

Chapter 9:
Connecting the Dots

Culture—the way people think, behave, and work in an organization—is difficult to control. Thankfully, that's not what this model asks of leaders. Leaders of an "All In" culture seek to *influence* culture versus *controlling* it. Because we humans are complex animals, developing a culture of excellence is time consuming, challenging work. Leadership is the key ingredient for success.

What we have learned in the preceding chapters is the absolute power of growing a Level 5 culture. The qualities of Level 5 individual leadership must transfer into the entire organization—and that's where the deliberate application of the Big 6™ comes in. At the various levels of leadership (front line, organization, and enterprise), teams of leaders embrace and collaborate to implement these principles. There must be a deliberate, focused effort to bring these qualities to life. And it will take time.

Connecting the dots from a loosely-tied collection of individuals (Level 1) through a confederation of somewhat committed people led by a few caring, dedicated leaders (Level 3), to a world-class culture of excellence where everyone is "all in" (Level 5) is *not* a linear progression.

Like the journey to individual leader excellence, the road to having a culture of "All In" will have setbacks. Changes in leadership, market conditions, growth (especially acquisitions) will all adversely affect the cultural growth of your organization—at least initially. Your task as leaders of the enterprise is to understand these dynamics at work and take action to mitigate, then overcome, their adverse effects.

General Stan McChrystal uses the analogy of the coral reef to describe the *resiliency* of a healthy ecosystem, versus the robustness of the Egyptian pyramids:

> Andrew Zolli, a resilience thinker and writer, uses the Egyptian pyramids as an example of robustness. The fact that they are still standing proves the pyramids are extremely robust—they have successfully resisted all the stressors the architects had in mind when building them: wind, rain, and the other anticipated degradations of time. But if an unanticipated stressor—say, a bomb—blew a pyramid apart, the structure would not be able to reassemble itself. A coral reef, on the other hand, survives hurricanes not by being robust, but through resilience. Storms will destroy a certain proportion of coral, but if the reef is a healthy size, it will regenerate in short order.[45]

It is, indeed, the resiliency of the Level 5 culture that sets it apart. Robustness is strengthening the structural components, like the ancient pyramids. Resiliency is the linking of those components so they can reconfigure and adapt to changing

---

45 *Team of Teams*, pp. 79-80.

conditions. That's a significant distinction in what separates enduring cultures from the temporary ones. In the Information Age we're in now, robustness is simply not enough. The healthy paranoia we've talked about can only exist in a healthy framework *if the team members believe they can handle uncertainty.* Resiliency gives them that confidence.

In my experience, most organizations need some help to navigate these waters. Having a meaningful relationship with an experienced, dedicated consultant team is a tremendous asset in making a successful journey to cultural excellence—in bringing the Level 5 culture to life. I'd recommend Level Five Associates (of course!), and realistically the key is to develop a long term relationship of trust with your consultant partner.

It's like having a doctor you believe in. When I needed total knee replacement on both knees a few years ago, I turned to my orthopedic surgeon and next door neighbor, Dr. Mike Niles, and asked for help. His skill changed my life—but I also trusted him and followed his guidance. With an organizational consultant, you're doing much of the same thing with the life of your company. Take the time to develop this relationship.

What are the most effective tools for your toolbox to establish, nurture, and lead your culture to grow to Level 5? Here are some proven methods which you can start using right away:

Audit Where Your Team Sees Your Culture Now

The process can take several forms. I like the simple, direct survey technique. Here's a 12-item survey you can conduct across your organization or in selected departments or levels of responsibility:

On a scale of 1 to 5, with 1 being "Strongly Disagree" and 5 being "Strongly Agree," circle your response to the following statements:

1.   I understand our azimuth and my role in it.

        1   2   3   4   5

2.   My responsibilities are clear and measurable.

        1   2   3   4   5

3.   My leaders do what they say they will do.

        1   2   3   4   5

4.   I can speak and be heard.

        1   2   3   4   5

5.   We operate in an environment of trust.

        1   2   3   4   5

6.   Our teams do the right thing when no one else is there.

        1   2   3   4   5

7.   Our leaders will not hesitate to accept responsibility.

        1   2   3   4   5

8.   We live in a world of mutual accountability.

        1   2   3   4   5

9.   My leaders understand and support balanced living.

        1   2   3   4   5

10.   We onboard new people to understand our culture.

        1   2   3   4   5

11.   We conduct effective meetings.

        1   2   3   4   5

12.   We take our work seriously, but not ourselves.

        1   2   3   4   5

Although not scientific, you can pretty well assess the heartbeat of your organization based on the scoring range of the survey. If your aggregate score (total for each person divided by the number of people in the survey) is in the range of 50–60, you've got a very healthy culture in place.

On the other hand, if your scores range from 12–20, there are some serious challenges out there you've got to address.

Make sure you look for trends in the responses—specific areas of weakness to focus on. Later, when you go back and conduct a subsequent survey, you can determine whether the programs you've put in place are working.

My experience in observing other organizations who use this survey is that you'll see different aggregate scores across the company as a whole, and in different departments and levels of responsibility. I'd recommend starting with the company as a whole. Afterwards, provide them with an aggregate set of results (this is an important part of the credibility of the survey process), and then commit to a set of actions to improve the areas where there are clear gaps or shortcomings.

Develop an Integrated Process Team
and Charter Them to Create an Alignment Plan

Select a diverse group of leaders and team members to establish an Integrated Process Team (IPT) to develop an Alignment Plan. This Alignment Plan will address specific areas of improvement for your culture, particularly those the audit identified as weaknesses. From my experience, the optimum size of the IPT should be 5 to 7 (if it gets much bigger it becomes unwieldly, and smaller it will be seen as not representative of the whole organization). Make sure they represent the major departments of your organization, so everyone feels they have some representation on the team.

Using some of the techniques in Patrick Lencioni's *Five Dysfunctions of a Team*, develop a pathway for the Integrated Process Team to build your Alignment Plan. Keep the workforce apprised of the team's progress. The senior leader in the company should be an ex-officio member of the team (so he doesn't vote on decisions, but he's aware of them and the process underway for making those decisions).

Publish the Alignment Plan
and Build It Into Your Operational Rhythm

With some degree of fanfare, publish the AP. Make it an event, with some positive publicity. The message is important here, and the workforce will be much more supportive of the AP if they know the leadership is enthusiastic about the journey the plan represents.

Ensure there is an established timeline for the various stages of the AP (usually the complexity of this type of program will drive the planners to establish phases of implementation). Keep the IPT on duty while the plan is implemented, so they can assess and adjust as you progress.

Develop a Culture Scorecard to track the AP. Based on the focus areas of the plan, one technique would be to use the Big 6™.

1. Set the Azimuth

2. Listen

3. Trust and Empower

4. Do the Right Things When No One is Looking

5. When in Charge, Take Charge

6. Balance the Personal and Professional

There are specific components of this scorecard for each principle. Here are some examples (and they are representative of others you and your team will develop to suit your organization's needs):

Set the Azimuth:
- Mission Statement review and approval
- Intent is codified with End State, Key Tasks, and Purpose
- Values review and approval
- Culture (behaviors) review and approval
- Culture (behaviors) embedded in performance objectives and appraisal
- Strategic Planning process implemented
- Onboarding Process implemented

Listen:

- High Value Meetings Agenda implemented
- Backbrief program implemented across departments
- One-on-One Meetings program implemented
- Cell phone training program implemented
- Body Language training program implemented

Trust and Empower:

- Decision Tree program implemented
- Mentor program implemented
- SMART (Specific-Measurable-Assignable-Realistic-Time Related) goal training program implemented

Do the Right Thing When No One is Looking

- Hero of the Week program implemented
- Best Practices program implemented to share success stories
- Handwritten Note program implemented

When in Charge, Take Charge

- Performance and Potential Assessment program implemented
- Talent Management program implemented
- Internal Leader Development program implemented
- Team Training program implemented

Balance

- Balance Assessment training program implemented

- Work Schedule Review program implemented

- Family Recognition program implemented

- Fun program implemented

Expect this Alignment Plan to show progress in stages, so you'll need some tactical patience and persistence to stay the course. If your scorecard system is designed to create monthly reports, you should be able to identify trends and charter the IPT to recommend adjustments as needed.

The key to success here is *commitment*. The process is not complex, but it will not work without the dedicated commitment of the leadership team, top to bottom. This is your opportunity—go for it!

If we can help, please contact us at **levelfiveassociates.com**. We have a dedicated team of professionals who have been there and done that, so we'll be happy to assist. Enjoy the journey!

About the Author

Major General (Ret) Robert W. Mixon, Jr. served for more than 33 years in the United States Army before co-founding Level Five Associates, a company with over 40 years of combined military, corporate, and not-for-profit senior leadership experience.

Robert has commanded an Army division and served as a senior corporate executive. The co-author of the Amazon Number 1 best seller, *Cows in the Living Room: Developing an Effective Strategic Plan and Sustaining It*, Robert is an active blogger, publishing articles and videos bi-weekly about his Big 6™ Leadership principles. He has taught leadership in executive

Major General (Retired) Robert W. Mixon, Jr.

education programs at the Simon Business School, University of Rochester, the Olin Business School of Washington University at St. Louis, and the Cox Business School, Southern Methodist University. In 2016, Robert was selected for a Teaching Excellence Award at the Cox Business School.

At the time of his retirement from active duty in the United States Army, Robert was Commanding General Division West, First Army and Fort Carson Colorado, having previously commanded the 7th Infantry Division. Throughout his career of over 30 years of active service, he commanded operational units at every level.

Robert also held critical staff positions, including serving as deputy executive assistant to General Colin Powell, the Chairman of the Joint Chiefs of Staff. Prior to his assumption of command of the 7th Infantry Division, he led the Army's Task Force Modularity, an integrated team of highly-skilled military and civilian experts chartered with changing the Army's force design while at war. The team accomplished the mission in less than one year, transforming our battlefield formations, which allowed the Army to dominate the enemy in both Iraq and Afghanistan.

Robert retired from active duty in October of 2007 and transitioned to Magnatag Visible Systems in Macedon, New York as its President. Under his leadership, the company successfully navigated through the worst economic crisis in America since the Great Depression. In 2009, he became Executive Vice President of CDS Monarch, a 501c(3) not for profit based in Webster, New York, providing life and job transition for over 1,500 people with intellectual disabilities. He also helped found the Warrior Salute Program for Veterans with Post Traumatic Stress and Traumatic Brain Injuries. To date, over 70% of the veterans entering the Salute program have successfully graduated and are living independently.

Today, Robert leads Level Five Associates, helping companies and organizations grow world-class cultures through developing leaders who 'get it' and building exceptional, high performing teams. Their clients range from both services and manufacturing sectors, as well as government agencies. He remains and continues to serve as the President of the West Point Class of 1974, and has served in a number of organizations serving Veterans and their families throughout the years.

He and his spouse Ruth live in Pittsford, New York, where they enjoy time with their two sons' families.